THE HOTEL MAINE.

HOTEL MAINE. TAAKENA
LADY COOKS,
FRESH FRUIT FISH & GAME
ALWAYS ON HAND,
NORMAN D. MACKINLAY PROP.

TALES OF AN
UNSUNG SOURDOUGH

TALES OF AN
UNSUNG
SOURDOUGH

THE EXTRAORDINARY KLONDIKE ADVENTURES OF JOHNNY LIND

PHIL LIND *and* **ROBERT BREHL**

● ●

PAGE TWO

To my granddaughter, James; grandson, Jack;

and all the great-great-grandchildren of John Grieve Lind.

The Lind Family torch has been passed to all of you.

Cataloguing in publication information is
available from Library and Archives Canada.
ISBN 978-1-77458-293-0 (hardcover)
ISBN 978-1-77458-294-7 (ebook)

All photographs courtesy of the
Phil Lind Klondike Gold Rush Collection,
Rare Books and Special Collections,
University of British Columbia Library

Page Two
pagetwo.com

Edited by Kendra Ward
Copyedited by Rachel Ironstone
Proofread by Alison Strobel
Jacket and interior design by Peter Cocking
Jacket photos courtesy of the Phil Lind
Klondike Gold Rush Collection.
Front jacket: RBSC-ARC-1820-PH-0743
Back jacket: RBSC-ARC-1820-PH-1255
Map by Jeff Winocur
Printed and bound in Canada by Friesens
Distributed in Canada by Raincoast Books
Distributed in the US and
internationally by Macmillan

23 24 25 26 27   5 4 3 2 1

Frontispiece: John Grieve Lind and a dog, in
front of a cabin in the Klondike, after 1896.
RBSC-ARC-1820-PH-1250
Facing page: Detail of a postcard depicting
Miles Canyon in Douglas, Alaska, between
1900 and 1920. RBSC-ARC-1820-PH-1789

CONTENTS

FACING PAGE: Three men on railroad tracks, 1898. Construction of the White Pass and Yukon Route railroad began in 1898 to provide access to the Klondike. It was completed in 1900. RBSC-ARC-1820-PH-0788

SUMMIT CHILKOOT PASS,   COPYRIGHT 189

PREFACE

FOR CENTURIES, dating back to ancient Roman times, the lure of gold has sparked mass movements of people. Gold rushes have been ignited on every continent.

One of history's most famous was Canada's Klondike Gold Rush of 1896 to 1899, when a hundred thousand people from all over the world set out to a rugged land with an incredibly harsh climate. The image of rivers and creeks filled with gold was compelling, especially to disillusioned and unemployed workers across North America during a depression at the end of the nineteenth century. But most of these stampeders were horribly ill prepared; and thousands perished along the way.

This book is about the little-known story of Johnny Lind—my grandfather—a railroader-turned-prospector from London, Ontario, who was already up north looking for gold when the big strike occurred in August 1896.

Ever since I was a little boy, I've heard stories about my grandfather's adventures. And I've been fascinated by the Klondike all my life.

Inspired and coaxed by my father, Jed, my grandfather's second son, about fifty years ago I began collecting first-edition books, diaries, letters, photographs, rare maps, newspapers, posters, and ephemera—anything that caught my eye involving one of the most colourful periods in North American history, the Klondike era.

There were few who collected Klondike material, and this remains so, but those who did, like I did, collected intensely. I visited antiquarian fairs across North America and developed a network of dealers, collectors, and traders of Klondike memorabilia from Anchorage to Vancouver, Portland to San Francisco, Toronto to New York.

The Klondike is such a fascinating story about huge amounts of gold—twenty million ounces found around two small creeks—that set off a worldwide stampede. It was about dreams, and, like life itself, it could be wonderful or it could be awful.

My collection grew into thousands of pieces and has been designated "a cultural property of outstanding significance" by the federal government's Department of Canadian Heritage. And it is my pleasure to donate the Phil Lind Klondike Gold Rush Collection to my alma mater, the University of British Columbia, to share with researchers and the public at large.

FACING PAGE: The Chilkoot Pass summit, 1898. When news of the gold rush broke, first in San Francisco and Seattle in 1897, thousands rushed to the North in search of fortune and adventure. On arrival, they faced arduous winter conditions. RBSC-ARC-1820-PH-0801

The collection includes more than five hundred books, 1,800 photographs, and seventy-four maps, as well as thousands of diaries and letters and other personal items from the people who went to the Klondike in the late 1890s and early 1900s.

Before moving into Johnny's story, it is worth pointing out that the Klondike had many common characteristics of other gold rushes: lots of people flocked, few struck it rich, most faced incredible hardship; lawlessness, mayhem, even murder ensued, as did disgraceful displacement and destitution of local Indigenous people.

The Klondike was also unique. Reaching the coveted goldfields was much more difficult here because of the hostile northern wilderness, mountain passes, avalanches, and treacherous icy waters, which were the only access back then.

For those who arrived first, the bounty of riches the Klondike offered came in all shapes and sizes: gold dust, gold flakes, leaf gold, coarse gold, gold nuggets, and more. Miners routinely found fifty dollars per pan, sometimes even $500 per pan. By comparison, the best pans of the California Gold Rush fifty years earlier produced thirty-five or forty cents of gold.

The gold was so plentiful that Klondike miners mistakenly viewed it as a renewable resource. In only a thousand days—the length of President John F. Kennedy's presidency, or half as long as World War II—the Klondike Gold Rush was effectively over.

Like a shooting star, the Klondike illuminated spectacularly on the world stage—"The Last Great Gold Rush," author Pierre Berton called it—before fizzling out in the blink of an eye. But the public's fascination with the Klondike never ended. And one of the best examples of this comes from a most unlikely source: a breakfast cereal company.

In 1955, almost sixty years after the Klondike Gold Rush ended, Quaker Oats was a sponsor of the popular American adventure television program *Sergeant Preston of the Yukon*. In a bid to sell cereal, a Chicago advertising executive, Bruce Baker, came up with the idea of giving away a deed to one square inch of land in the "Yukon gold rush country." Quaker Oats bought nineteen acres of land near Dawson City for $1,000, divided it up into twenty-one million tiny pieces, and stuffed the deeds into cereal boxes. Quaker Puffed Wheat, Quaker Puffed Rice, and Shredded Wheat sold like hotcakes thanks to the deeds to one inch of Klondike land. It was one of the most successful commercial publicity campaigns of the twentieth century.

Interestingly, the Canadian government repossessed the Quaker land in 1966 because of $37.20 in back taxes.

As a testament to the staying power of the Klondike legend, even today Yukon officials still receive letters, emails, and phone calls about the deeds. The land office of the Yukon currently contains an eighteen-inch-thick file folder of correspondence regarding the promotion.

The allure of the Klondike remains more than 125 years later.

A NOTE ON THE CURRENCY CONVERSION

PUTTING A value on the twenty million ounces of gold extracted from the Klondike in today's dollars is tricky.

The price of gold at the time was about $20 per ounce (or $600 per ounce today, because $1 then is roughly equal to $30 now). That would put the dollar value of Klondike gold in the late 1890s at around $400 million—or $12 billion in today's currency. But investment firms and gold experts often peg the number at about $34 billion in today's dollars and prices. The discrepancy comes down to these words: *in today's dollars and prices.*

Although the price of gold fluctuates, it is currently trading at a price about three times higher than its price during the Klondike Gold Rush when the present value of money is accounted for.

A better way to imagine this is if twenty million ounces of gold were discovered today, its value would be $34 billion.

But, back then, the Klondike miners converted virtually every ounce of gold into dollars. And that is an important distinction: few ounces of Klondike gold were kept and handed down to descendants, who today could cash it into dollars at three times the price the miners did. Therefore, the more accurate estimate of Klondike gold is $12 billion, not $34 billion. Still, a lot of money over a short period of time.

These calculations get even trickier when factoring in that gold, not dollars, was the local currency in the Klondike until May 1898, when the Bank of British North America opened in Dawson City, followed by the Canadian Bank of Commerce. Every saloon and restaurant had scales, not cash registers. Bags of gold dust or nuggets were used as poker chips. Gold paid for food, supplies, and the companionship of women. When the kings of the Klondike played high-stakes poker, they'd sometimes bet upwards of five pounds of gold on one hand—and that would translate into *$50,000* today.

Even after the arrival of banks, gold was the predominant Klondike currency until 1899, when most prospectors rushed off to Nome, Alaska, for another strike.

For the purposes of this book, when a conversion is cited, it will be based on the 30-to-1 scale, since those with gold had to spend it or convert it into dollars at some point.

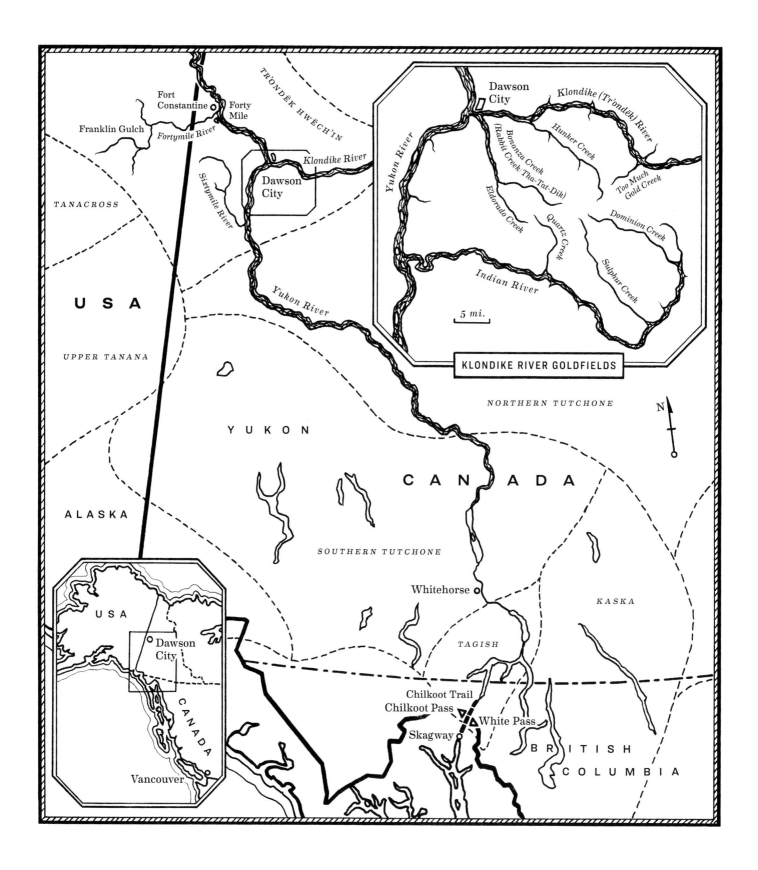

Fort Constantine
Forty Mile
Franklin Gulch
Fortymile River
Klondike River
Dawson City
TRONDËK HWËCH'IN

KLONDIKE RIVER GOLDFIELDS

Dawson City
Klondike (Trǒndëk) River
Hunker Creek
Bonanza Creek (Rabbit Creek/Tha-Tat-Dik)
Too Much Gold Creek
Yukon River
Eldorado Creek
Quartz Creek
Dominion Creek
Sulphur Creek
Indian River
5 mi.

TANACROSS
Sixtymile River
USA
UPPER TANANA
YUKON

NORTHERN TUTCHONE

N

CANADA

SOUTHERN TUTCHONE
ALASKA

Whitehorse

KASKA

TAGISH

USA
Dawson City
CANADA
Vancouver

Chilkoot Trail
Chilkoot Pass
White Pass
Skagway

BRITISH COLUMBIA

TIMELINE

FEBRUARY 8, 1867: John Grieve Lind (more commonly known to friends and family as Johnny Lind) is born in Pond Mills, near London, Ontario. He is one of eleven children—nine girls and two boys. Johnny's twin brother, George, is minutes older than him.

1883: At age sixteen, Johnny heads to the United States and lands a job working with the Great Northern Railway Company across the northwestern states.

APRIL 26, 1894: After flipping a coin—heads, travel north in search of gold; tails, head south to Venezuela to find his fortune in oil—Johnny leaves for Tacoma to begin a journey north.

MAY 3, 1894: A steamer, the S.S. *City of Topeka*, drops Johnny Lind in Alaska.

MAY 7, 1894: After travelling the treacherous Chilkoot Pass, Johnny arrives back in Canada and begins a long river journey to the outpost of Forty Mile.

EARLY JUNE 1894: Johnny arrives at Forty Mile, procures supplies, and explores nearby creeks for gold.

JUNE 12, 1894: Finding no luck around Forty Mile, Johnny leaves for Franklin Gulch, Alaska, about one hundred miles upriver, or southwest, on Fortymile River.

JUNE 21, 1894: Johnny reaches Franklin Gulch. After working for other miners for a few weeks, he buys his first claim from a veteran prospector who is leaving to explore elsewhere.

JULY 1894 TO DECEMBER 1896: Johnny works tirelessly around the creeks in Franklin Gulch. He accumulates a wealth of knowledge about placer gold mining (extracting gold from sand or gravel), acclimatizing himself to the hard, cold environment, and even finding some gold—not a lot, but enough for him to begin buying claims in the Klondike when he arrives there.

AUGUST 16, 1896: A Tagish man, Keish (Skookum Jim Mason), travelling with his sister Shaaw Tláa (Kate Carmack); their nephew Káa Goox (Dawson Charlie); and Shaaw Tláa's husband, American prospector George Carmack, discovers gold in the Klondike.

DECEMBER 1896: Johnny arrives in Forty Mile for supplies and discovers the town has been deserted. He learns of the huge strike in the Klondike in August 1896. He and his business partner Skiffington Samuel "Skiff" Mitchell head to the Klondike.

JANUARY 1897: Skiff and Johnny begin buying pieces of staked claims and mining them for gold.

JULY 1897: The treasure ships *Excelsior* and *Portland* arrive in San Francisco and Seattle, respectively, with massive amounts of Klondike gold, igniting the outside world's stampede to the Klondike.

JULY 1898: Johnny leaves the North for first time since May 1894 and returns to his family's farm near London, Ontario.

MAY 1899: Johnny returns to the Klondike with his sisters Wilhelmina and Adah, who will soon marry his two business partners, Skiff Mitchell and Johnny Crist, respectively.

1901: Johnny leaves the Yukon for the last time and never returns. He lives another forty-six years.

(1)
LEGACY
OF A
SOURDOUGH

A COLD, RUGGED PLACE SHAPED
A WARM-HEARTED MAN

FIFTY YEARS AFTER the Klondike Gold Rush, in a church 3,700 miles southeast of Dawson City, grown men in cement-dust-covered overalls stood in solemn silence, tears running down their cheeks.

FACING PAGE: Box Canyon on the White Pass and Yukon Route, 1900. A feat of engineering at the time, the railway ran around 110 miles, from Skagway to Whitehorse, and was among the steepest routes in North America. RBSC-ARC-21-10-PAGE-31

In St. Marys, Ontario, they were attending the funeral of John Grieve Lind, in St. James Anglican Church, a Victorian-era stone edifice. None knew him from his years in the North, but many had heard his Klondike tales and knew how the cold, rugged place shaped him into a warm-hearted man with a genuine soft spot for those less fortunate.

It was 1947, and John Grieve Lind had succumbed to a stroke at age eighty.

A month after my grandfather's funeral, I would celebrate my fourth birthday. Our lives barely intersected. I have no first-hand memories of him. I am told he did kindly grandpa things like rocking me to sleep on his lap and walking me to the park.

Because of my young age, I was not at his funeral. But my mother, who loved and respected her father-in-law, told me about that day many times. The level of detail in her description always impressed and moved me.

Using money he had earned in Klondike gold, John Grieve Lind, along with wealthy investors from Toronto, founded St. Marys Cement Company, which would grow into the largest independent cement company in Canada. The hard-working, burly men in the church were his employees, although in "people terms" they were more than that to him. In today's corporate-speak they'd be called "stakeholders," "partners," "company builders," or some other twenty-first-century HR buzzword.

To John Grieve Lind, they were friends, associates, even extended family. He knew everyone at the plant by name as well as where most of them lived in St. Marys and surrounding Perth County. During the darkest days of the Great Depression, he found ways to prevent laying off a single person. He opened a line of credit at the local store and told the proprietor to put the groceries on his account if anyone didn't have enough money for food.

That's the kind of man John Grieve Lind was, and these tough-as-nails men in the church held genuine affection for him. Without changing out of their work clothes, they had hustled from the cement plant for the hour-long service. In the church, they stood with their backs against the walls instead of sitting in pews next to more formally attired mourners, lest they dirty their suits and dresses. Some openly wept; others pulled out cloth handkerchiefs as if trying to conceal their emotions; others vigorously joined in the hymns. After the funeral, the men walked back to the cement plant a few blocks away to finish their shift.

As a young boy, the story of the men at my grandfather's funeral was imprinted on me. My grandfather treated all employees with respect. In life, I have a feeling, he enjoyed the company of blue-collar types even more than that of starch-collared folks. This preference stemmed from the Klondike and the back-breaking work in relentless pursuit of gold under incredibly harsh conditions.

John Grieve Lind's passing stirred so much emotion in so many diverse people. He was revered and respected in St. Marys by both hard-working labourers and the upper crust. High-ranking businesspeople from Toronto and London travelled to St. Marys for the funeral. The local newspaper, the *St. Marys Journal*, ran an account of his life on the front page, from top to bottom over two columns, under the headline "St. Marys Cement Co. Head John G. Lind Passes." It is extremely rare, even for a small-town newspaper, to devote so much space on the front page to one person's death. The article begins by calling him St. Marys' "most prominent and colourful citizen," which is quite something considering the retailing Eaton family started in St. Marys and another St. Marys native was the ninth prime minister of Canada, Arthur Meighen. Retailing patriarch Timothy Eaton was long dead, and his family relocated to Toronto, but Meighen was very much alive when John Grieve Lind's passing was

chronicled in the *St. Marys Journal*. "John Lind will be remembered by his fellow citizens of St. Marys as the robust, smiling, keen-faced gentleman who always wore a black Stetson hat, and enjoyed a good cigar," says the newspaper. And "as the man who believed in honest toil, a good job of work and who encouraged the building of fine parks and a community spirit in this town."

Wanderlust and Railroading

To understand Johnny Lind's part in the Klondike Gold Rush, let's consider for a moment what we know about his humble beginnings and his life before his northern adventures.

John Grieve Lind was born February 8, 1867, five months before Canada became a country. He was one of eleven children: nine girls and two boys. His twin brother, George, was minutes older than him, and the boys were in the middle of the family as the fifth and sixth children. The older girls were Jane (or Jennie, born 1858), Ann (1862), Jessie (1863), and Margaret (1865). The younger girls were Mary (or Minnie, 1870), Agnes (or Aggie, 1871), Adah (1874), Ellen (or Ella Belle, 1877), and Wilhelmina (1880).

Parents Adam and Ann Grieve Lind hailed from Scotland and married in 1857, when Adam was twenty-eight and Ann twenty-two. They ventured to Canada shortly after the wedding. Desperately poor, the family lived in a small farmhouse and worked a one-hundred-acre farm near Pond Mills, today a neighbourhood in southeast London, Ontario.

Not interested in farming, teenaged Johnny Lind was filled with wanderlust and adventure. After grade eight, he dropped out of school. At age sixteen, he headed down to the United States and, in 1883, landed a job working with the Great Northern Railway Company. The Great Northern was controlled by the famous railroad magnate James Jerome "J.J." Hill, who was expanding across the northwestern United States, from the Great Lakes to the Pacific Ocean, during the late nineteenth century.

Johnny Lind and J.J. Hill had more than a few things in common. Hill was also born in Ontario, near Guelph, albeit thirty years before Johnny. Both left school early but continued self-taught learning throughout their lives. Like Hill, Johnny Lind was adept at geometry, land surveying, mathematics, and engineering. Both had a voracious appetite for hard work. At Hill's railroad, Johnny quickly rose to foreman of a crew of two hundred men. He became proficient in designing and overseeing the construction of trestle bridges over rivers, canyons, and gullies. In essence, he became an engineer without the papers. This was one of many self-taught skills he would acquire over the years.

Not a lot is known about this railroad period of Johnny's life. We do know he was based in Missoula, Montana, for at least the last five years of his railroading career. Sitting smack dab where five mountain ranges converge, Missoula is often described as the "hub of five valleys." At this time of Johnny's life (unlike his time in the North), he doesn't appear to have kept a journal or diary. And letters home, if any, are lost to the Lind family. What is known is that at age twenty-seven, with more than a decade of railroad and engineering work under his belt, he was anxious for a new adventure, one that would profoundly change his life and the lives of so many in the Lind family.

Grandfather loved Missoula, this western Montana town, for its beauty and its fishing, a passion he passed down to many of his descendants, including me.

Johnny Lind's formal schooling ended at grade eight, but his education was the school of learning through experience. And he attended classes every single day. Whether building railroad trestles and bridges or sluicing for gold in northern riverbeds, his experiences in business, engineering, and mining prepared him well for the Klondike Gold Rush.

BEFORE THE GOLD RUSH

PROSPECTING THE NORTH

BEFORE MOVING ON to Johnny Lind's northern adventures,
a few words about the years immediately preceding the Klondike Gold Rush
and before Johnny Lind's arrival.

FACING PAGE: Prospectors packing over the Chilkoot summit route, 1897.
Miners relied heavily on Tlingit and Tagish packers to carry
their provisions over the rugged Coast Mountains. RBSC-ARC-1820-PH-1255

On March 30, 1867, the United States purchased Alaska from Russia for $7.2 million (or roughly $127 million today). Cash poor at the time, Tsarist Russia believed that the United States owning Alaska would counterbalance and offset any designs of Russia's then-greatest rival in the Pacific, Great Britain, in the region. From the American perspective, the acquisition ensured the United States' access to the Pacific's northern rim.

After the California Gold Rush of 1849, prospectors began moving north following other gold rushes in places like Colorado, the Dakotas, and, of course, British Columbia, especially the Cariboo Mountains region where the big Barkerville gold strike occurred in 1861. As each gold rush dissipated, prospectors trickled farther and farther north. To the prospectors, the rugged northern land was remote, the climate severe, the geography uncertain, and the boundaries hazy between Alaska, Yukon, and northern BC. (Indeed, Yukon was at that time a district within the North-West Territories and would not become its own territory until 1898 during the height and frenzy of the Klondike Gold Rush.)

The year 1873 marked the arrival of three men who formed a partnership that would be vital to the Klondike Gold Rush in the late 1890s. They were Irishman Arthur Harper and Americans Captain Al Mayo and LeRoy Napoleon McQuesten, known simply as "Jack." The trio set up a network of trading posts in the Yukon and Alaska, often providing "grubstake"—materials and provisions supplied to prospectors in return for a share in the resulting profits. They owned a steamboat called the *New Racket*, which Captain Al guided up and down the Yukon River for many summers and which was a lifeline to the outside world for food, supplies, mail, and other items.

"Without these three men, and a fourth named Joseph Ladue, who arrived a decade later, the series of events that led to the Klondike discovery would not have been possible," writes Pierre Berton in *Klondike: The Last Great Gold Rush, 1896–1899*. "Without the string of posts they set up along the Yukon, the systemic exploration of the river country could not have taken place."

Integral to the endeavours of McQuesten, Mayo, and Harper were the Indigenous women who married them, helping them survive on the land and enabling their trading by acting as go-betweens and translators with local Indigenous groups. Satejdenalno (Katherine McQuesten), a Koyukon woman from the village Kokrines, married McQuesten in 1878. She was fluent in Russian, Koyukon, and English and acted as an important translator for McQuesten and other traders, including Mayo and Harper. Neehunilthnoh (Margaret Mayo), whose family came from the Koyukuk and had settled in the Yukon before he arrived, married Mayo in 1874. In that same year, Seentahna (Jennie Harper, née Bosco), a first cousin of Neehunilthnoh, married Harper. All three women raised several children, some descendants of whom still live in the Yukon today.

Joseph Ladue was a prospector, businessman, and founder of Dawson City. He had a reputation as a "promoter," someone whose words had to be taken with a

grain of salt. Harper, Mayo, and McQuesten were pioneers, prospectors, and traders known for their honesty and integrity, and as men without fear of anything. As agents for the then-monopolistic Alaska Commercial Company, they traded with Indigenous Peoples and supplied grubstake to prospectors during a series of smaller gold rushes in the Yukon Valley throughout the 1880s and 1890s.

My grandfather got to know all these men. On his first trip north, Johnny met Harper at a trading post near the mouth of the Pelly River on the Yukon River. Some 155 miles upstream, Harper had lost all his sugar in the Whitehorse Rapids. "He had no sugar, but had honey, which we bought," grandfather writes in his journal.

As my grandfather and his mates continued their journey downstream, they went days without anything sweet, so decided to make camp and have a treat that evening. But just as they were reaching shore, the Yukon River turned turbulent and all the honey they'd just purchased "fell into the raging river, and sank before our eyes."

My father, Jed, told this story whenever he was asked to describe the conditions my grandfather endured. Imagine the disappointment. A year's supply of honey swallowed up by the mighty Yukon River and not knowing when they might taste something sweet again.

Harper, McQuesten, and Mayo's first post was Fort Reliance, located on the east bank of the Yukon River about six miles downstream, or north, of what would one day become Dawson City. McQuesten and his assistant, Frank Banfield, established Fort Reliance in 1874 with consent from a group of Hän-speaking Tr'ondëk

Hwёch'in people, particularly Chief Gäh St'ät (Catsah, also known as Abraham Harper), who selected the site for them. For the entrepreneurial Tr'ondёk Hwёch'in, accomplished traders who had been obtaining European goods through First Nations such as the Tanana and the Gwich'in for decades before their first encounters with white people, having the trading post within their traditional territory was an advantage. It gave them easy, unencumbered access to European trade goods. It was a joint living and trading site—there were both Tr'ondёk Hwёch'in pit-houses (a type of semi-subterranean winter dwelling) and settler-style log buildings. Fort Reliance became a major landmark for traders and, later, prospectors. For example, settlements and rivers, such as Fortymile and Sixtymile (both tributaries of the Yukon River), were named for their distance from this fort.

The Yukon—which comes from the word "Yu-kun-ah," meaning "great river" in the Gwich'in language—is the longest river in Yukon and Alaska and, by many measures, the third-longest in North America, after the Mississippi and Mackenzie Rivers. Its source is in northern British Columbia in the Coast Mountains, mere miles from the Pacific Ocean. It flows north and west two thousand miles before it "sees" the Pacific again when it empties into the Bering Sea, itself a part of the Pacific. Think of the majestic river as the shape of a giant horseshoe that travels through Yukon and then Alaska. To understand the river's dominance over northern geography, its watershed's total drainage area is 330,000 square miles—almost the size of British

Columbia, minus Vancouver Island. It was the principal means of transportation for Indigenous Peoples, traders, and prospectors.

By the mid-1880s, an estimated two hundred miners had taken the Chilkoot Trail from Dyea, Alaska, crossing the treacherous Chilkoot Pass into British Columbia and then onward, into the Yukon. Mining camps popped up throughout the Yukon Valley, which extends well beyond Yukon territory and into Alaska. The first camp of significance was near the mouth of the Stewart River, a tributary of the Yukon, where placer gold (extracted from sand or gravel) was discovered in 1883. Placer gold—sometimes called "free gold"—refers to the auriferous mineral that over time has been ground into dust and nuggets and can be mined by any person with a shovel, a pan, and a strong back.

In 1886, prospectors fled Stewart River and headed northwest to Fortymile River, where larger gold deposits were discovered. The camp at Stewart River became a ghost town overnight, and the outpost of Forty Mile flourished for a time, becoming the Yukon's first official town. (To distinguish between the town and the river, Fortymile is spelled as one word when referring to the river.) This kind of story repeated itself many times in Alaska and Yukon as prospectors migrated to where gold was found.

Fortymile is of interest for many reasons, not least of which is that it is the first river on which Johnny Lind looked for gold, beginning in June 1894. Established in 1886, the town had stores, and bars, as well as an Anglican mission and the Yukon's first day school for

Indigenous Peoples, which was later absorbed into the residential school system. But Forty Mile was largely a community of hermits whose common bond was that they were all dreamers in search of gold and were content, for the most part, with isolation from the outside world. Miners typically lived with their mining partners in tiny cabins with windowpanes made of empty pickle jars or liquor bottles. A wood-burning stove was their only source of heat. The endless, dark days of winter could see temperatures fall to forty degrees below zero and stay there for weeks.

Communities like Forty Mile thrived on unwritten laws—often called the Miners' Code. During this period, they had no elected mayors or councils, no lawyers, judges, police, or jail. The code was wide-ranging and applied to things like using anyone's uninhabited cabin, which was allowed at any time, although it was expected to be cleaned up and a supply of fresh kindling left behind. Men shared their good fortune, and when gold was discovered, news of it was expected to be immediately spread to other miners.

When someone broke the code, a miners' meeting would be convened and justice meted out, often harshly. The accused would have his say, as well as the accusers. Punishment could range from lenient (repay a debt or be granted a divorce) to severe (the lash, hanging, or immediate banishment from the community, which could lead to a brutal death in the wilderness).

Such was the environment in Yukon and Alaska in the two decades leading up to the great discovery in the Klondike, southeast of Forty Mile, where the Klondike River joins the Yukon River, on August 16, 1896. Things were, however, beginning to change even before that landmark date.

The trio of Harper, McQuesten, and Mayo went their separate ways in 1893. Harper partnered with Ladue and ended up in business at Forty Mile and surroundings with trading posts, sawmills, and other businesses. McQuesten founded, and settled at, Circle City in Alaska, 170 miles downstream (northwest) of Forty Mile. Mayo ended up even farther downstream in Alaska, past Stevens Village at the mouth of Minook Creek. Harper and his wife, Seentahna, separated permanently in 1895. Sadly, Harper—nicknamed "Hard Luck Harper" for his lack of prospecting success—made a fortune with his landholdings in Dawson but died of tuberculosis in Arizona in November 1897 before he could enjoy his newfound wealth. McQuesten was the most financially successful of the three; he died in California in 1909, survived by Satejdenalno, who managed their ample estate until her death in 1921. Mayo, the only one to live out his days in Alaska and Yukon, died in 1924. His wife, Neehunilthnoh, died two years later.

Another big change was afoot in the area in the early to mid-1890s. Law and order was on its way, at least on the Canadian side of the border. Colonel Samuel B. Steele, superintendent of the North-West Mounted Police, forerunner of Canada's iconic Royal Canadian Mounted Police, hatched a plan to bring a semblance of order to the last frontier. In 1894, he dispatched Inspector Charles Constantine, the first Mountie to enter the Yukon, along with one sergeant.

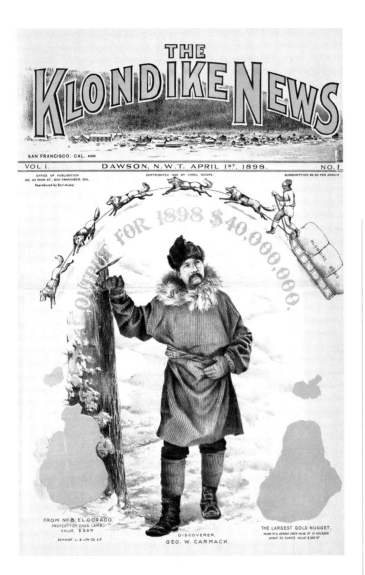

Cover of the first issue of *The Klondike News*, April 1, 1898. RBSC-ARC-1820-27-02

original inhabitants of the region." The inspector's first report back to the government showed no evidence that he was aware that the Tr'ondëk Hwëch'in, for instance, were, as Dobrowolsky points out, "leading self-sufficient lives far from the settlements."

One final note (of which greater detail can be found on pages 48–49) is about the distinct cultural differences between American and Canadian mining communities. Namely, the Canadian camps ceded to authority more readily, whereas the Americans held on to their local customs and rules much longer, even well past the Klondike Gold Rush. In general, Americans didn't want foreigners mining in Alaska. Canada, on the other hand, happily accepted non-Canadian prospectors so long as they paid 10 percent royalties to the Canadian government.

A Word about Truth and the Gold Discovery

On August 16, 1896, a Tagish man, Keish (Skookum Jim Mason), and an American prospector, George Carmack, hit a bonanza on Rabbit Creek in the Klondike. The two men were travelling together that day with Shaaw Tláa (Kate Carmack, who was Carmack's common-law wife and Keish's sister), and Káa Goox (Dawson Charlie, their nephew).

Because of his massive ego, and likely racism, too, Carmack was determined to set the "official" history that he was the discoverer. As the only white person in the group, he filed the first claim, known as Discovery claim, and he alone broke the news of the gold at a saloon in Forty Mile, which set prospectors scurrying to the creek,

They established Fort Constantine, just across the river from Forty Mile. A year later, a detachment of twenty men joined Constantine, who set out to abolish miners' meetings wherever he found them on Canadian soil. Helene Dobrowolsky notes in *Hammerstones: A History of the Tr'ondëk Hwëch'in* that Constantine had also been instructed by the Canadian government to ascertain the situation of Indigenous Peoples in the Yukon, "but to avoid any compensation or action on their behalf. The Canadian government expected the Yukon to be a short-lived mining camp and was unwilling to make any long-term commitments to the itself a tributary of the Klondike River, to stake their claims. Over the remaining twenty-five years of his life, Carmack promoted himself as sole discoverer.

Johnny Lind was a twenty-nine-year-old man and about 150 miles away when the Klondike gold was discovered. He was too late to stake an original claim on Rabbit Creek, which was soon renamed Bonanza Creek, but he was there to buy pieces of many claims, long before tens of thousands of stampeders arrived from the four corners of the world between 1897 and 1899. However, Johnny did not buy the widely accepted story of the day and decades after—that George Carmack discovered the gold that ignited the Klondike Gold Rush. In a document he wrote in the 1930s about his days in the North, he makes his beliefs clear.

In this unpublished Lind family heirloom, he writes, "While the gold discovery was made in August 1896 by Skookum Jim, George Carmack and Tagish Charlie, Carmack took all the credit for it, as the other two were [Tagish]." Note Johnny mentions Keish (as Skookum Jim) first, and before Carmack. He adds, "They went up the wrong creek and while eating lunch, Jim knelt down to get a drink of water and saw the bed of the creek literally covered with gold nuggets. This caused the stampede, probably the largest ever."

***

My grandfather referred to Keish as Skookum Jim Mason and may not have even known his Tagish name. "Skookum" is a Chinook jargon word that means strong or excellent. Keish earned his nickname after carrying

156 pounds of bacon over the snow-covered summit of the Chilkoot Pass for William Ogilvie, the government's chief surveyor, who determined the boundaries between Yukon and Alaska.

I am proud that my grandfather did not toe the party line of the day and that he properly credited the likely real discoverer of the Klondike gold, long before so many others.

***

In *Gold Diggers: Striking It Rich in the Klondike*, Charlotte Gray writes that George Carmack took credit for the discovery because, "as he told his brother-in-law, nobody would believe a Tagish man."

Today, historians usually give the credit for the discovery to Keish. Deb Vanasse notes in *Wealth Woman: Kate Carmack and the Klondike Race for Gold*, that, at the time, there was "even talk that Kate [Carmack] played a role in plucking the first nuggets from the creek." Yet the *Canadian Encyclopedia* online says: "Gold was discovered in mid-August 1896 by George Carmack, an American prospector, Keish... and Káa Goox... Tagish First Nation members into whose family Carmack had married." Thus, Carmack is still credited as the primary discoverer.

"Of course, we will never know for sure the events surrounding the discovery as everybody later wanted to claim a hand in it," writes Michael Gates in the *Yukon News* in 2013, but he shares Johnny's belief: the discovery belongs to Keish, who did stake his claim at 1 Below Discovery.

A COMPLEX HISTORY

For time immemorial, Indigenous Peoples had been living in the Klondike and surrounding areas. Life for Indigenous Peoples in Alaska and Yukon had been changing throughout the nineteenth century because of the presence of Russian and British fur traders and a smattering of prospectors, mainly Americans. Relative to what happened during the Klondike Gold Rush, these changes were modest.

In the two decades leading up to the gold rush, the Tlingit of Southern Yukon-Alaska, protecting their fur trade interests, regulated how many prospectors entered the area by guarding inland routes, namely the Chilkoot Pass and the White Pass, to the rivers and creeks where miners sought gold. Miners paid Tlingit and Tagish men and women to carry their provisions over the Coast Mountains. If the packers were busy, miners would have to wait or outbid others for services.

Beginning in 1897, hordes of newcomers (mostly white men, a handful of Black and Asian men, and a few women) arrived seeking fortunes. It is estimated that a hundred thousand people stampeded north and approximately forty thousand reached the newly established Dawson City and the nearby goldfields. And the stampeders were not about to wait to get inland. They clogged the trails, hauling their own provisions. They clear-cut trees for the wood necessary to build rafts, cabins, and sluice boxes to sift gold from muddy water. They brought diseases like influenza, smallpox, and tuberculosis, among other perilous illnesses. They thought nothing of the fish, otters, and beavers in the murky brown waters their constant digging churned out. They staked claims and built the saloons, hotels, homes, and businesses of Dawson on a floodplain—a swampy moose pasture—across the Klondike River from Tr'ochëk, a traditional seasonal fishing camp of the Tr'ondëk Hwëch'in people. The stampeders overran and destroyed Tr'ochëk, which eventually became known as Klondike City, or "Lousetown" because it housed the red-light district.

The original inhabitants of the Klondike region, a diverse group of families descended from Hän, Northern Tutchone, and other language groups, were perhaps the most impacted by the gold rush. Craig Mishler and William E. Simeone note in *Han: People of the River (Hän Hwëch'in)*, "The Klondike Gold Rush was the defining moment in Han history. More than any other event, it transformed the economy, society, and culture of the upper Yukon Valley and subordinated the interests of the Han to those of the mining industry and majority non-Native society."

The Tr'ondëk Hwëch'in assisted the gold seekers in many ways, for example, supplying meat, fish, and other resources, as well as winter wear. Over the longer term, however, they suffered from the environmental damage of the gold mining on the rivers and forests, as well as from the creation of Dawson. The gold rush brought chaos and dislocation.

The Tr'ondëk Hwëch'in population had already begun to decline after the discovery of gold along Fortymile River in the 1880s but it dropped steeply after their move to a reserve, a result of the contaminated water supply and numerous epidemics, including smallpox. They found few ways to benefit economically from the sudden colonization that was brought by the gold rush, and their fishing and hunting grounds were largely destroyed.

Candice Hopkins, a curator and writer of the Carcross/Tagish First Nation, and whose great-grandmother was a niece of Keish, suggests the complex implications of her ancestor's discovery of gold in her essay "The Gilded Gaze: Wealth and Economies on the Colonial Frontier."

Just before the gold discovery on Rabbit Creek that set off the last great gold rush, Keish had a dream about a frog with gold disks as eyes. "For Tlingit people, the frog signifies wealth," Hopkins writes. "Keish knew prosperity would soon follow. Yet he couldn't shake an unsettled feeling. When the frog turned to look at him, he was overcome with a great emptiness: in that instant he saw the entire human world transfixed by its gilded gaze."

After waking at dawn the morning of August 16, 1896, "Keish mumbled greetings in Tagish before heading down to the creek to wash his face in the cold water," she notes. "After focusing his eyes, he saw them: three nuggets, each the size of a dime." When he returned to camp to show the others, Carmack shouted for joy, danced a jig, and posted a sign by the creek, staking his claim.

"With the planting of a sign, the power structure was transformed," Hopkins writes. "Indigenous hosts were now guests in their own land. A kind of colonialism set into motion—not settler colonialism, as at this stage most of the newcomers had no intent to stay, but *extractive* colonialism, based on the acquisition of resources."

The antique books in the Phil Lind Klondike Gold Rush Collection reflect writers' sentiments during that time. The literature places Indigenous Peoples mainly on the margins, often in a negative light, or simply ignores them. Only over time is the wider world coming to understand the impact of the gold rush on First Nations people's lives, land, and culture, as well as recognizing the significant roles the Indigenous Peoples played: laying out the best routes to the goldfields and hauling tons of supplies; helping build boats and rafts for the Yukon River; teaching survival skills for the harsh climate; supplying traditional clothing like mukluks, mitts, and parkas; and hunting and supplying wild game during food shortages.

Yukon Indigenous Peoples, and in particular for this story the Tr'ondëk Hwëch'in people, survived the onslaught of the gold rush and the sudden, severe colonial experience it created, and they now work to educate settlers about how to properly live on this land today. Two excellent resources for a broader understanding of the gold rush and its aftermath, from Indigenous sources and knowledge keepers, are the Dänojà Zho Cultural Centre in Dawson City and the Dawson City Museum.

(3)

JOURNEY
TO THE
GOLDFIELDS

AN EXTRAORDINARY TALE
OF ADVENTURE AND HARDSHIP

AS THE LILAC, columbine, and lupin began to bloom
in 1894, Johnny Lind stood in Missoula, Montana, and flipped a coin.

FACING PAGE: Gold miners climbing to the summit of Chilkoot Pass, 1898. In 1894,
when he arrived in the North, Johnny Lind took this now-legendary route through
Alaska and northern British Columbia on his way to the Yukon. RBSC-ARC-1820-PH-1774

If heads turned up, he would travel north in search of gold, if tails, he'd head south to Venezuela to find his fortune in oil. Heads it was. The simple fate of a coin toss. Had it come up the other way, who knows what would have happened? What can be said for certain is that twenty-seven-year-old Johnny Lind then embarked on his first trip north during the spring of 1894. It is an extraordinary tale of adventure and hardship.

My grandfather kept handwritten journals, which were meticulously collected, copied, and typed out by a family member ninety years after he wrote them. The late John King, who was married to my first cousin Margaret King (a Johnny Lind grandchild like me), typed them out, with the spelling and grammatical errors intact, in 1983.

Where the journals are quoted directly, I have amended spelling mistakes scribbled out by a young man of great fortitude, whose education ended at grade eight.

On April 26, 1894, Johnny boarded a Northern Pacific Railroad train bound for the West Coast, on his way to Alaska-Yukon and the goldfields. On the NPR train, Johnny jotted down bittersweet feelings in relation to moving on and abandoning his railroad-building colleagues, and he compared it to leaving home a decade earlier. "After being acquainted with them for five years or more, the friends one leaves only gives place to new friends and acquaintances."

A couple of days later, he arrived in Tacoma, Washington, where he boarded the S.S. *City of Topeka*, a thirty-year-old 1,057-ton passenger steamer that the Pacific Coast Steamship Company ran up and down the coast between San Francisco and Alaska. A young writer, the renowned novelist Jack London, would later travel on the *City of Topeka* on his way north, as did many other Klondike characters. London didn't find gold—and almost died several times, including from a severe case of scurvy—but he mined the Klondike for stories that he eventually turned into countless bestselling adventure books. Likewise, a year after Johnny Lind had been aboard, the legendary Klondike businesswoman Belinda Mulrooney worked as first stewardess on the *City of Topeka* for two years, beginning in 1895. Foreshadowing what lay ahead for Mulrooney in the Klondike, she quickly branched out into retail sales, providing both necessity and luxury items to passengers travelling on the ship.

Returning to Johnny Lind's voyage, after a short three-hour trip up to Seattle, the *Topeka* docked for a five-hour layover. Johnny went ashore and picked up much-needed supplies for his northern trip.

His food included 250 pounds of flour, one hundred pounds of bacon, fifty pounds of beans, twenty pounds of coffee, ten pounds of salt, ten pounds of sugar, and ten pounds of baking powder. Other supplies were two frying pans, a bucket, six tin plates, six knives, six forks, six spoons, four tin cups, two picks, two shovels, two gold pans, two axes, one whipsaw, a hammer, and ten pounds of nails, all of which added up to almost five hundred pounds. (Although Johnny's journals make

no mention of a rifle and ammunition, he later mentions hunting geese, grouse, and duck, and shooting a black bear.)

Johnny returned to the *Topeka*, and the ship set sail for Alaska. The next morning from the top deck, Johnny marvelled at the beauty throughout the Strait of Georgia, an arm of the Salish Sea between Vancouver Island and the extreme southwestern mainland coast of British Columbia "where the islands are very numerous and the boat nearly touches some of them...the trip up the BC coast...is magnificent and entrancing."

I, too, fell in love immediately with British Columbia in the early 1960s as a university student. The province is
the most fascinating place in the world to me. I learned later that I come by this affinity honestly since my grandfather wrote similarly about it in his journal, which I read for the first time some twenty years after graduating from UBC. It gave me a warm feeling.

During his seven-week journey to the goldfields, Johnny Lind hit his first rough patch when he got terribly seasick just north of Vancouver Island and south of Haida Gwaii, on the waters of Queen Charlotte Sound. "The water was extremely rough, [but the] scenery here very grand and imposing," he writes. In hindsight, he'd find seasickness the least of the hurdles he needed to conquer.

Over the years, I've fished a couple of dozen times near Haida Gwaii and off Prince Rupert. The water can be quite rough and tempestuous, the weather harsh.

<hr>

On May 3, 1894, Johnny arrived in Juneau, Alaska, which he describes as a "quite large town." This gives readers an indication of the remoteness all around him. According to the 1890 US census, Juneau had a population of 1,253; the census breaks down the population in Juneau at that time into five categories: "White [671], Mixed [43], Indian [527], Mongolian [11], and Others [1]." (It should be noted that the term "Indian" refers to Indigenous Peoples, and the term "Mongolian" likely refers to people of Asian descent. These terms are considered offensive today.)

<hr>

My first impression of Juneau was much different than my grandfather's. I was a fifteen-year-old boy on a youth excursion trip with my pal Cammy McArthur and some kids and adult guides from the United States in July 1959. I collapsed on the sidewalk, violently ill. An emergency appendectomy at the little hospital in Juneau saved my life. Like my grandfather before me, I dodged the grim reaper while north.

<hr>

From Juneau, Johnny and some other men from the *Topeka* hired an Indigenous man and his large canoe to take them the eighty miles up the Lynn Canal (an inlet, not an artificial canal) to Dyea, Alaska, the jumping-off point to the Chilkoot Pass. This portion of his trek took thirty-six hours, including eleven hours marooned on a sandbar waiting for the forty-foot tide to return. It was cold, rainy, and foggy. His food was nicely packed away, and he dared not dig into it under those conditions. Once at Dyea, with the tide out again, "we had to carry our ton of provisions to high land, through mud and salt water, for about a quarter of a mile and with it still raining," Johnny writes without a tone of complaint or grumbling.

The following day, May 5, Johnny and his party headed out on the Chilkoot Trail, the entry into Canada, first through northern British Columbia and then Yukon. (The journals don't mention how many men there were, but one of Johnny Lind's future gold partners, Johnny Crist, was in the party.) On May 6, 1894, they made "Sheep Camp"—the last rest stop before ascension to "Stone-House," the summit of the Chilkoot Pass, known as such because it looks like an enormous old castle from a distance.

A few things must be pointed out here about the Chilkoot Pass. First, since Johnny Lind arrived in 1894—three years before the stampede—he had a somewhat easier time than stampeders who followed because Tlingit and Tagish guides were available for hire, to pack and carry the prospectors' supplies to the summit. Before the 1880s, the Tlingit closely guarded the Chilkoot Trail as a traditional and important trade route that could be crossed year-round. Leading up to the gold rush, more prospectors came to the area, and the Tlingit faced mounting pressure to allow foreigners to use the Chilkoot Trail, the best-known and most-used route across the mountains and on to the goldfields. Prospectors using the trail understood that Tlingit and Tagish packers must be hired to move expedition gear.

Johnny writes that he paid the Tlingit packers "one dollar a pound to pack our plunder (and haul it) to the summit of the Pass." From there, the Tlingit departed and the prospectors "sledded our stuff downhill to the head of Lindeman Lake." A conservative guess at the weight of Johnny's gear by this point would place it at four hundred pounds, which means he paid $400. That is the equivalent of $12,000 in today's money—all in the relentless pursuit of that shiny metal!

Once the stampede of tens of thousands of people descended upon Dyea and nearby Skagway (the gateway to the White Pass), there were scant Tlingit to hire, and they were excellent bargainers, charging high prices for packing. Many stampeders couldn't afford them and had to haul everything themselves, often making numerous trips up and back. The job could take a month or more, depending on the time of year and the amount of supplies. By 1897, the Mounties also insisted that stampeders have a ton of supplies before entering Canada. Ensuring each person had a year's worth of food was an attempt to prevent starvation—but it also significantly added to the burden of carrying supplies up and down the passes.

Regardless, when a person travelled the two passes, crossing the Coast Mountains was no walk in the park.

The thirty-three-mile Chilkoot Trail and Pass was a much steeper climb, but the somewhat flatter White Pass was longer at forty-five miles. As one stampeder put it: "There ain't no choice, one's hell and the other damnation." Or, as the great Klondike writer Tappan Adney notes, "Whichever trail you took you wish you had taken the other."

To get a sense of the horrors and struggles faced by these stampeders, one need only view the hour-long award-winning 2015 documentary The Klondike Gold Rush, *which aired across North America on the PBS television network. It is available, free of charge, online.*

The horror stories on the trails from gold rush stampeders are well documented. Johnny himself mentions a couple. One is about an old prospector named Bill Stewart returning north mere days after Johnny Lind crossed the Chilkoot Pass. A blizzard quickly stormed through and the savvy Stewart knew what to do immediately. "He had the presence of mind to throw down his pack, get his robe and a small tarpaulin to cover himself," Johnny writes. "He was there for nine days with only raw oatmeal to eat and some tallow candles."

Also in the spring of 1894, Sid Wilson and John Reid, both miners Johnny came to know, were stuck on the Chilkoot Pass for ten days. They had dogs, which they cut loose from their harnesses and never saw

again. On that cold, windy mountain for ten straight days with little to eat, they would have been constantly pushing off the snow accumulating on their tarps so as not to be buried alive. The fear. The hunger. The loneliness. The uncertainty of survival. "This is supposed to be the stormiest Pass in the world," Johnny writes of the Chilkoot Pass. "There is never two or three hours at a time that it does not snow or blow. The only water one could get was from snow, which must be melted by lighting candles under your frying pan. Many a man perished here."

Fortunately, Johnny and his party crossed the Coast Mountains in four days and arrived at Lindeman Lake, then at Bennett Lake and the headwaters of the Yukon River on May 10, 1894. Over those days, snow blindness struck. Also called arc eye or photokeratitis, snow blindness, which is essentially a sunburn of the cornea, is not permanent but is painful and disorienting, especially when climbing and descending mountain trails.

Johnny Lind writes that he was "blind as a bat" and had to be led by the arm for the last two days of the trek.

At Bennett Lake, it was time to build a boat, even though Johnny's "eyes [were still] pretty sore." They cut down a tree and began "sawing lumber for [a] boat." Although the size of his party is not known, Johnny writes that "one of the boys killed a goose and it was quite a treat."

By May 16, the sun was warming, some snow was melting, and Johnny's eyes were no longer stinging. After a week at Bennett Lake, the boat was finished and they launched it at Caribou Crossing, just inside the Yukon, on May 20.

The party was headed to Fortymile River, a tributary of the Yukon River, "which by the way is 600 miles farther on." Imagine the determination and courage to carry on? Where there was ice, they'd drag the boat. Where there was open water or slushy snow, they would use poles to keep moving the boat forward.

Packers ascending the summit of the Chilkoot Pass, May 1898. Snowy conditions persist on the pass well into spring. Stampeders arriving by the thousands faced a steep climb, often in fierce conditions.

RBSC-ARC-1820-PH-0804

PACKERS ASCENDING SUMMIT OF CHILKOOT PASS.
COPYRIGHT 1898 E.A.Hegg.

On Bennett

"We poled for fifteen hours today," Johnny casually writes of this arduous task. Some days they advanced as little as three miles, and other days, when the water was brisk, they'd go seventy or eighty miles.

The journal entry for Friday, May 25, 1894, is fascinating for what it *doesn't* say: "Started by boat down the river. A fine large river, lots of waterfowl every place we go on open water. Ice running bad in places. My partner John Crist and myself run the canyon in an eighteen-foot boat." The canyon Johnny refers to is Miles Canyon, just south (upriver) from the Whitehorse Rapids. The formidable canyon is about a mile long and only fifty feet wide—with a large whirlpool spinning halfway through. Its walls push the water into the centre, churning up roaring, foaming, lashing waves that would have created terror for anyone trying to navigate while preventing a boat from smashing into the hard basalt walls.

Johnny and Crist were faced with a difficult choice: they could brave the white water with all their supplies on board and be through in minutes, or they could unpack the boat and portage around it, which would take days. Johnny makes no mention of the risk, or even how he and Crist made the dreaded decision to roll the dice. Perhaps, like Hobson's choice, they concluded that in this case choice was an illusion. It was worth the risk to get through in minutes. And yet, Johnny was rather nonchalant in stating that they simply ran the canyon where many stampeders would later perish, as Tappan Adney and Jack London would both write. It must have been a harrowing five minutes for Johnny and Crist.

This unmitigated courage and steel will to get on with things constantly amazes me about my grandfather. The day after navigating Miles Canyon, he portaged around the Whitehorse Rapids "on account of rocks." Just too much risk, soldier on, he seems to say.

Today, we have so many modern conveniences, but for my grandfather it was all back-breaking work like navigating rapids, poling through slow-moving water, or sledding the boat on ice for twenty miles. He does mention one luxury: "Lots of moose meat to eat and [we] are happy."

By the way, the Whitehorse Rapids are no more after the construction of a dam in the late 1950s that created Schwatka Lake.

———

On June 5, 1894, Johnny notes: "One peculiar thing is it never gets dark here." He simply would never have thought about the Earth's tilt, but being just below the Arctic Circle there would be nearly twenty-four hours of sunlight each summer and almost twenty-four hours of darkness each winter.

Along their way to the goldfields, they stopped at a couple of trading posts on the banks of the Yukon River to pick up supplies. "Everything expensive," he writes, adding a "very common" pair of shoes was $8 and corn syrup $3. Today, that $8 would be $242 and $3 would be $91. Paying $242 for a pair of shoes may be on par with the cost of some contemporary footwear, but have you ever paid $91 for a bottle of corn syrup?

Then, on June 9, tragedy struck. Cold, wet, and tired, the group hit roaring waters on the Yukon near

Sixtymile River. Johnny's boat lost some supplies—including the container of honey—but other boats fared worse. "Several of the other boats lost their all," Johnny Lind writes. "Two men drowned."

By the middle of June, a mere seven weeks after that coin toss in Missoula, Johnny reached Fortymile River, one of the most fruitful gold-producing creeks found prior to the Klondike Gold Rush. Here Johnny planned to begin his hunt for gold.

At Fortymile River was the small hamlet called Forty Mile. Full of Sourdoughs (the name for miners and prospectors who had spent a full year in the region), it was fifty miles northwest of the site that would become Dawson City, which didn't yet exist in 1894. At the time, Forty Mile was a collection of log cabins, other edifices, and a bustling trading post run by Jack McQuesten and Al Mayo. "Two finer men never lived," Johnny writes.

The day after his arrival, Johnny Lind tells a story about a man and a horse floating on a raft along the river into Forty Mile. A group of Indigenous people congregated at the river's shore, transfixed by the sight of the horse, an animal they had never before seen. When the horse came ashore and started neighing and galloping, they startled, although, Johnny notes with admiration, they "would, without fear, hunt wolves, bears, caribou or a bull moose, [which] when wounded is rather vicious."

Johnny identifies the man on the raft with the horse: "Little Alex McDonald." Indeed, Alex McDonald went on to earn the nickname "King of the Klondike," one of the richest prospectors and businessmen, who amassed

(and lost) a fortune estimated between $7 million and $27 million. Today, that would be between $200 million and $800 million! Nova Scotian Alex McDonald was a giant of a man, commonly referred to as Big Alex in many texts. "Because of his size and awkward movements, McDonald was known as the Big Moose from Antigonish," says Pierre Berton in *Klondike*. Yet Johnny refers to him as "Little Alex."

———

For several generations, the Lind family has given people nicknames that are the opposite of the person's character or build. My uncle John was an extraordinarily strong, brawny man, but he was tagged with the name of the famous Swedish opera singer Jenny Lind his entire life. My father, Walter, a tall skinny kid, was always called Jed after the rotund bus driver at his school, Ridley College in St. Catharines, Ontario. Even my first cousin Margaret was known as "Mike."

And here is my grandfather calling the future King of the Klondike "Little Alex McDonald." It is quite a coincidence.

———

So it was that, after seven harrowing weeks, Johnny Lind arrived at last at Forty Mile, the oldest town in Yukon. He'd overcome seasickness and snow blindness; felled trees and built a boat; poled or pulled the boat for hours and miles, day after day; lost supplies and witnessed death in rough river waters.

Now, the truly hard work was to begin.

A GOVERNED TERRITORY AND A WILD COUNTRY

During the years before the Klondike Gold Rush, the Canada-US border was blurry and the culture of non-Indigenous newcomers consisted of Russian, British, and French traders, missionaries, and explorers. The stampede changed all that, with protruding differences appearing in Canadian and American communities.

In 1867, Canada became a country and the United States bought Alaska from Russia. During the ensuing years, American prospectors began to spread into the North, along with some Canadians and miners from Europe.

By 1895, a thousand white men and two or three dozen white women newcomers in Alaska and Yukon carried on as if the cartographer's borderline between Alaska and Yukon did not exist, nor the laws of either country. Instead, the prospectors lived by the Miners' Code and meted out justice as they saw fit.

The code was simple: no stealing; share food; tell every other man about any precious metal discovery; and, most importantly, do unto others as you would have them do unto you.

Miners' meetings would come together as a sort of vigilante court whenever a man had a grievance. A chairman would be appointed, evidence heard from both sides, and the remaining men would act as jury with one vote each. Rulings and punishments were final and applied immediately. Minor offences such as claims disputes were solved through reimbursement. Major offences such as stealing would result in hanging or banishment, which amounted to pretty much the same thing, as surviving alone in the wilderness was unlikely.

In 1894, the North-West Mounted Police sent Inspector Charles Constantine and a sergeant to the Yukon Valley, but in such a vast area, two officers could do little more than send reports to Ottawa of bootlegging and other purported crimes. By early 1897, six months after the gold strike, there were still fewer than two dozen officers trying to maintain law and order across the enormous wilderness. Not until 1898 did the Mounties dispatch Colonel Samuel B. Steele and two hundred men to the Yukon.

On his way to Dawson City, Steele waited six weeks in Skagway, Alaska, for the bulk of his men and supplies to arrive by boat. "Skagway with 70 bars, a bevy of bordellos, and schemers fleecing dreamers was the roughest place in the world, little better than a hell on earth," Steele wrote in his 1906 memoir *Forty Years in Canada*. Chronic criminal Jefferson "Soapy" Smith and his gang of 150 ruffians, confidence men, and swindlers ran the town and the lawless trails heading into Canada. One of Soapy's men even shot and killed a US Marshal during a saloon fight, only to get off at trial with a plea of self-defence.

When Steele did arrive on the Canadian side of the border, differences between the two countries emerged. Steele was determined to fight lawlessness in Canada and keep mob rule away. One way he did this was by forcing those entering

View of a winter camp, after 1897. A group of women and men, including law enforcement, pose outside tents while woodsmoke billows out of makeshift chimneys. In 1898, the Canadian government sent hundreds of Mounties to establish its hold in the North. RBSC-ARC-1820-PH-0282

Canada's North to bring a year's worth of food and supplies. This not only increased food supplies for the exploding city of Dawson, but it also limited the influx of stampeders by turning away thousands who were ill prepared.

Miners' meetings were banned in Canada, but not in Alaska. A "Wild West" environment persisted in the US territory, and the limited law enforcement officers there seemed to look the other way when it came to vigilante justice and mob rule.

Another way to look at it is that the Klondike was a place where law-and-order Canadians attempted to co-exist with more unruly Americans on Indigenous lands. But make no mistake, during the gold rush, the biggest festivities in Dawson City were held on July 4, not July 1, then known as Dominion Day. There were far more Americans than Canadians in the Klondike.

And similar to today, there were many cultural differences between Canada and the United States in the Klondike period, apparent when one scratched below the surface.

4

BECOMING A SOURDOUGH

MINING NEARBY IN ALASKA, 1894 TO 1896

WHEN IT comes to Johnny Lind's ultimate gold-mining success, it is impossible to overstate the importance of the period from the summer of 1894 to Christmas of 1896—even though for him it had nothing to do with the Klondike.

FACING PAGE: Two men stand outside a cabin, after 1897. RBSC-ARC-1820-PH-0237

Instead, he was about 150 miles from the Klondike, in Alaska. But these years were crucial to him for three vital reasons.

First, he adapted to the harsh climate; both the brutally cold, long, dark winters and the ravages of mosquitoes and blackflies that drove many cheechakos (the name the Indigenous packers called the northern novices that approximately translates as "tenderfoot newcomers") to the edges of insanity.

Second, Johnny learned so much about placer gold mining: panning, burning to the bedrock, building sluice boxes, and a whole lot more. Not that he needed a lesson in hard work, but he got that, too, from the daunting digs and grinding eighteen-hour days.

Third, he found some gold—not a lot, by comparison, and he doesn't reveal exactly how much in his journals—but it was enough for him to buy pieces of staked claims in the Klondike once he arrived at the end of 1896.

In a nutshell, 1894 to 1896 made Johnny Lind a true Sourdough.

The miners' nickname "Sourdough" dates back to 1849 California, because sourdough was the main bread eaten during that gold rush. Indeed, sourdough bread remains a staple of San Francisco culture today, with many international chefs and gourmands believing the world's best sourdough bread is baked in the Bay Area. The nickname followed prospectors north with one addendum: in Alaska and Yukon, a miner had to last at least one full year, and especially to survive the winter, to be called a true Sourdough. That's because during

the coldest months of the year, a prospector protected their sourdough bread starter, or leaven, by keeping it close to the body, usually in a small container hung around the neck, to keep the yeast warm and active.

A few weeks after their successful and gruelling trek north, Johnny Lind and his business partner, Johnny Crist, decided to leave Forty Mile. In June 1894, after hearing about gold finds in creeks and gulches (ravines with fast-moving creeks) upriver in places like Miller Creek, Nugget Gulch, Glacier Creek, and Franklin Gulch, they pushed about one hundred miles southwest on the Fortymile River.

With supplies packed, they headed out by boat, poling and paddling against the current. The Fortymile, a major tributary of the Yukon River, is known for its twisting and tortuous route through the rugged mountain forest landscape. There are many blind turns and severe rapids like what they experienced on the Yukon River. The two Johnnys ended their first day just before the Canyon Rapids, where they set up camp.

At 3 a.m., in the dusky light, they were awakened when an old Sourdough named Frank Buteau, travelling with two Indigenous women, stumbled upon their camp. The three were lost in the woods and hadn't eaten in more than twenty-four hours. Johnny Lind cooked them up some food and listened to Buteau's tales of gold. The old Sourdough had originally come from Quebec but had been in the North for more than a decade. Buteau told Johnny Lind and Johnny Crist that, at Miller Creek, two or three men had taken out $100,000 worth of gold that spring, or $3 million in

today's currency. The news heartened the two Johnnys, enforcing in them the feeling that they were heading in the right direction.

But getting beyond the oncoming Canyon Rapids would take several days "of the most arduous work, wet all the time," Johnny writes, "climbing over rock and wading and pulling very hard and discouraged with mosquitoes that were murderously torturing us."

After resting up for a couple of days, Johnny Lind and Johnny Crist made their way to Franklin Gulch, where about twenty miners were looking for gold. It is here that they met Skiff Mitchell, a prospector born in St. Stephen, New Brunswick, but who called California home.

———

Like Johnny Crist, Skiff Mitchell would partner with my grandfather and remain friends all their lives, even becoming family.

———

Skiff and Johnny had a special relationship. As Johnny's son Jed Lind writes in an undated letter penned several years after Johnny Lind's death, "My father frequently boasted of the partnership the two of them shared— [with a motto] 'share and share alike.'... They kept a common purse, which would only work, it seems to me, based on complete trust and an absence of frivolity and dissipation on the part of both and mutual confidence." No other partner held such a position in Johnny's heart and mind. "Curiously enough, my father's other partner

John Crist did not seem to hold or gain my father's esteem to the same extent," Jed Lind notes.

———

Perhaps my uncle Jenny embodied this rapport between Johnny and Skiff: Uncle Jenny's real name was John Skiffington Lind.

As an example of this special relationship between Skiff and my grandfather, my father, Jed, mentions an annual undisclosed sum John Grieve Lind paid Skiff in California in the years after the Klondike. As executors of their father's will, Jenny and Jed Lind determined the money must have been some sort of dividend in St. Marys Cement.

However, Skiff was not an official shareholder of St. Marys Cement and there was no record that he ever owned shares. "There were no records to show Skiff had invested, but he may have just the same, or, more probably, Dad had notionally 'given' him shares which Dad continued to hold," Jed Lind writes, adding, "it could also have been the case that Dad's active partner [in St. Marys Cement], Alfred Rogers, did not see a place for an absent stockholder."

Regardless, this "share and share alike" bond between the friends was taken to the grave by Grandfather.

———

At Franklin Gulch, after several weeks working for others, Johnny Lind bought a claim belonging to a man named Bender, "an old horse thief from little Rosebud, Montana." Bender had heard the gold rumours about

Miller Creek and headed there. Ever the entrepreneur, Johnny seized the opportunity to own a claim and work it himself.

Throughout the autumn of 1894, Johnny worked hard. He cut timber. He built sluices and flumes to separate gravel and gold. In other words, he was developing an operation of panning on a grand scale, not one pan at a time. He constructed a small dam to control the flow of water in preparation for the next year's spring runoff. "We were busy until the middle of November when we went to the Trading Post for our year's supplies," Johnny writes.

With the river frozen up, Johnny and a partner (likely Johnny Crist or Skiff Mitchell) made the trip back to Forty Mile in only three days. Here they heard news from the outside world and shared news from Franklin Gulch. They met men who had mined all over the world: from nearby BC and the US Rockies to Australia, New Zealand, and South Africa. "Really, all able, fearless men willing to take a chance on anything," writes Johnny, adding that they had some of the most colourful names, such as Tin Kettle George, Handshaker Bob, Windy Jim, Kaiser William, Red-Handed Mike, Slobbery Tom, Sorehead Ramsay, Swiftwater Bill, Stillwater Willie, and Sailor John. Surnames were optional.

The partners stayed in Forty Mile for more than two weeks, during which time Johnny witnessed the Miners' Code up close. On one occasion, an Englishman and a Frenchman were fighting over an Indigenous woman, and a duel with Winchester rifles was set for the morn. A miners' council of ten men with rifles, led by a president named Neal McArthur, was convened to ensure fair play for the duel. As the meeting progressed and rules were laid out, McArthur picked up about fifty feet of rope and slung it over his shoulder. The Englishman asked what the rope was for, and McArthur responded, "To hang by the neck the winner." Hearing that, the combatants mutually called off the duel, and both men, who were deemed to be troublemakers, were told to gather up some supplies and leave camp for good.

In another example of rough justice, a man was caught stealing bacon and butter in mid-winter, when everyone in Forty Mile was under food rationing orders. Some wanted him hanged there and then. The miners convened and heard from both accuser and suspect. The thief was deemed guilty and given ten days of provisions, a sleigh, and a rifle and ammunition. Calling it "almost a death sentence," Johnny reports that the man apparently got upriver almost 250 miles, nearly dead from starvation, and was rescued by a group of Indigenous people. He lived and hunted with them and never returned to Forty Mile.

Just before Christmas in 1894, Johnny Lind and his partner left Forty Mile to return to Franklin Gulch. With only one dog per sled to transport a year's supply of food, mining tools, and some new clothing, the journey took the better part of three weeks.

At the end of December, it would be utter darkness at all times, except between 10 a.m. and 3 p.m. when there was some light—mostly dusk-like. Each day, they'd stop to set up camp before absolute darkness.

"Of all the gruelling hardships, probably there is nothing that will sap the energy as freighting [supplies] with the temperature constantly at 45 to 65 degrees below zero," Johnny writes. After setting up makeshift tents—spruce branches with robes draped over them—the travellers would get a fire going to melt snow for water and to cook flapjacks. "Sometimes bacon," Johnny notes, "but it was usually so hard frozen that it could not even be chopped with an axe."

After eating, they'd wrap as many things around them as possible under the spruce boughs, and in the downright cold and snowy conditions, some nights, Johnny reports, he would be "too tired to sleep."

From whatever sleep they did manage, they'd awake in the deep darkness of 4 a.m., pack up, harness their dogs, and be travelling from 5 a.m. until about 2 p.m., when they'd set up their next camp before dark. "The time did appear endless, the cold intense," he writes. And then, finally, "At last, Franklin Gulch, and we both thought that never did our poor log cabin appear so inviting and cozy to us."

To explain the hardships my grandfather endured in pursuit of gold, my father often told the story of his losing a year's supply of honey in the Yukon River rapids.

I sometimes think that that three-week winter journey back to Franklin Gulch may have been the most severe test my grandfather faced, and there were plenty of other harsh tests.

———————

From January to May, the main job was what was called "burning to the bedrock"—under the banks of creeks and rivers. Using dry timber, every night miners would light fires to heat and thaw the ground. The next day, any unfrozen ground, called "pay dirt," would be shovelled out and moved to nearby ditches that had been dug in the fall, above the anticipated spring high-water mark.

With dams they'd constructed to control the next spring's runoff, miners would use the fast-moving spring water to pick up pay dirt and run it through sluice boxes to separate dirt, gravel, and gold. Wooden sluice boxes, or a slightly sloping wooden trough, were typically a foot wide, twelve feet long, and another foot deep. Each sluice box would be connected to another box six inches higher or lower to use gravity to sift the pay dirt, almost like the water in a slide at a water park moves people down.

But unlike a waterslide, the sluice boxes have riffles. These were important pieces of wood placed transversely along the bottom of the sluice to cause the water to eddy into small basins, impeding the current so that gold would settle and get trapped. It is quite ingenious, and Johnny Lind used this time in Franklin Gulch to learn such best practices.

And he learned from one of the best. One of his teachers in the Gulch was the old prospector Bill Stewart, who as mentioned had the wherewithal and savvy to hunker down on the Chilkoot Pass for nine days during a blizzard that killed other less-experienced men.

"The romance, if any, from placer mining is minimized by the extremely laborious work in connection with it," Johnny Lind writes. "One never knows with any assurance what the reward will be. Sometimes the pay streak is narrow and twisty and when off the pay streak you get very little gold for your work, but one always expects to get far more than one really does get. I suppose that is so in everything one attempts. At least, it has been in my experience."

Johnny Lind repeated this daily work over and over in Franklin Gulch for two years, and he became the first miner to sink a shaft all the way to bedrock on Chicken Creek, a fast-moving stream that runs through Franklin Gulch. He dug so deep and removed so much pay dirt that he hit igneous, metamorphic, sedimentary, and volcanic rocks below the permafrost.

By the way, Johnny Lind was one of the men who gave that creek its name. "We named the creek Chicken from the fact that the gravel was mostly the size of chicken feed," he writes.

Armed with knowledge and expertise in placer gold mining, acclimatized to the harsh environment, and with gold nuggets in his pouch, Johnny Lind was on the cusp of striking it rich in the Klondike. No longer a cheechako; he was a battle-hardened Sourdough.

GOLD FEVER AND OTHER AILMENTS

Untold thousands of stampeders perished just trying to get to the Klondike; from drownings on high seas or in fast-moving rivers to being buried by avalanches and dying of exposure on the trails. And still more died in the goldfields and in Dawson City from disease.

Scurvy, typhoid, dysentery, tuberculosis, bronchitis, sexually transmitted diseases, meningitis, and pneumonia all took a toll on Klondike fortune hunters. Scurvy, a vitamin C deficiency resulting from the limited diet of the three Bs—bacon, bread, and beans—"killed more stampeders than accidents on the Chilkoot Pass or in the mines," writes Charlotte Gray in *Gold Diggers*.

Jack London, only twenty-two at the time, and before his famed writing career, barely survived scurvy. Flat broke, London was given rations of grated potato, a little lemon juice, and spruce-needle tea—the only available sources of vitamin C—by a compassionate priest, William Judge, who also massaged London's inflamed joints brought on by the scurvy.

"Lassitude overwhelmed Jack," Gray writes. "His teeth loosened, his joints ached, his gums bled. When he pushed his thumb into the puffy skin of his legs, the dents remained. Months without fresh vegetables had produced the first signs of scurvy, or 'blackleg,' as Klondike stampeders called it because it turned men's legs dark purple with bruises."

Father Judge nursed hundreds of scurvy patients like London at St. Mary's Hospital in Dawson City, but the kindly priest succumbed to another Klondike malady—pneumonia. He died in January 1899 at the age of forty-eight.

Typhoid was another major cause of death. Many stampeders became sick with typhoid in dirty and cramped cabins and in Dawson City, a boomtown built on a swamp, with insufficient water and sanitation capabilities. Typhoid, a waterborne illness, is characterized by a high fever, diarrhea or constipation, and a rash. The bacteria, transmitted in contaminated water and food, would cause victims to become delirious and lose all energy, lying with eyes half-closed in a "typhoid state."

The lack of sanitation also led to many cases of dysentery, a disease in the intestines that results in bloody diarrhea, fever, abdominal pain, and dehydration.

Stampeders even became sick from watered-down liquor. Usually considered a safe bet to ward off infectious illness, liquor was so watered down in Dawson that bacteria multiplied in bottles of booze. One wag noted that by the end of the winter in 1898, "bars had been serving what amounted to whisky-flavored water."

Beyond the harsh climate and vast wilderness, oft-rampant diseases were another danger faced by stampeders, all of whom suffered from that gold fever dubbed by newspapers at the time as Klondicitis.

FACING PAGE: **St. Mary's Hospital, Dawson, Yukon Territory, between 1900 and 1920.** RBSC-ARC-1820-PH-1663

St. Marys Hospital Dawson Y.T.

5

OFF TO THE
KLONDIKE

AN EXPERIENCED MINER AT THE EPICENTRE OF THE GOLD RUSH

JUST BEFORE Christmas 1896, a twenty-nine-year-old Johnny Lind
arrived back at Forty Mile, along with Skiff Mitchell,
after four days of sledding in extreme cold weather of -60°F.

FACING PAGE: A man tends to his dogs on the ice, circa 1897 to 1903. RBSC-ARC-1820-PH-1741

Back in those days, the Fahrenheit scale was used and -60°F translates to -51°C. The Fahrenheit and Celsius scales intersect at forty degrees below zero.

Their plan was to pick up supplies and return to Franklin Gulch, where they had left ten thousand feet of whipsawed lumber for sluice boxes and other implements for placer gold mining. Things were getting exciting and a major expansion of their operations in the gulch was in the works for 1897. Or so they thought.

The once bustling town of Forty Mile, with a dozen or so lively saloons and round-the-clock poker games, was unrecognizable to the young men. "The Post was nearly deserted, as everyone was up at the Klondike," Johnny writes. "No one talked of anything else. Bonanza, Eldorado, Gold Bottom, Too Much Gold, and Hunker were the [creeks] most talked of."

Something else was new to Johnny at Forty Mile: there had been changes at the North-West Mounted Police barracks and stockade. In his previous visit, Johnny had met Inspector Charles Constantine, the first Mountie sent to Yukon, late in 1894. By 1896, Constantine had a contingent of about twenty men under his command and the manpower to enforce the ban on miners' meetings on Canadian soil in the area. "A finer body of men would have been hard to find anywhere," writes Johnny, who became a friend to Constantine and remained so even after the Mountie was transferred out of the Klondike in 1898. Indeed, Johnny organized a gift from the miners to Constantine for his service—a belt with a solid gold buckle.

Those were much different times. It is doubtful that a Mountie, or any government official, today would accept such a gift. In the thank-you note, Constantine writes, "Dear Johnny… The parcel arrived all safe. It is a very beautiful piece of work, and the sentiment prompting the donors is and will be highly appreciated by both Mrs. Constantine and myself… Believe me. Yours very truly, C. Constantine."

Returning to the deserted Forty Mile, Johnny Lind didn't hang around too long listening to the stories about gold in the Klondike. "Skiff Mitchell and myself could not stand it any longer and proposed to see for ourselves." The pair set out for Dawson City, fifty miles southeast, up the frozen river. The first day out from Forty Mile, Johnny and Skiff came upon a woman with a sleigh and a dog pulling a load of supplies far too heavy for only one beast. The woman was disoriented, hungry, exhausted, and cold.

As you'll read later in another poignant story— about the birth of Edna Eldorado—Johnny and Skiff were both wired to do the right thing. Knowing it would add hours to their journey to the Klondike, they cut the woman's dog loose and loaded her and her supplies on their sleigh behind their team of dogs and headed for Fort Reliance, an old trading post about ten miles from Dawson. With their team of dogs struggling with the extra weight, Johnny and Skiff pushed

when needed. They travelled all night and arrived at the trading post around 9 a.m. "That was the longest night I ever put in," Johnny writes.

At the post, they went immediately to a cabin with a stove belching out black smoke. Four people were huddled around the fire with food warming on the stove. They made way and put the frozen stranger near the fire, and she recovered nicely after a rest and a meal. Johnny and Skiff then headed out to finish their journey to Dawson and its nearby gold-filled Klondike creeks.

"We arrived in Dawson and found a great many of our gold mining friends were already in the field, and all agreed that this was possibly the richest gold find ever discovered," Johnny writes. "Some of the stories were rather exaggerated, but under the circumstances could be forgiven. Never was there so much excitement."

One can feel the enthusiasm in his words. Johnny and Skiff must have felt over the moon as trusted mining friends told them stories about all the gold, "the motherlode." But, no doubt, a massive feeling of disappointment would soon follow, after finding out all the creeks had already been staked and were being worked in preparation for spring cleanup when the gravel and dirt would be separated from the nuggets and gold dust.

A claim consisted of five hundred feet up and down the valley. Every claim was staked based on where the gold was originally discovered—the Discovery claim, which did not have a number. The first claim downstream on Bonanza Creek was known as 1 Below Discovery and the first claim upstream was known as 1 Above, and so on.

Eldorado, a tiny creek flowing into Bonanza, was initially shunned by the gold seekers. Only those who were too late to stake a claim on Bonanza Creek bothered with this little pup. However, as luck would have it, this little pup turned out to be the richest ground in the Klondike. Since the discovery of gold was on Bonanza, Eldorado claims did not have Above and Below claims, just 1 Eldorado, 2 Eldorado, 3, et cetera.

First things first: Johnny and Skiff researched and learned that many of the claims were staked by cheechakos—tenderfoots—who just happened to be around when George Carmack arrived at Forty Mile to announce the great Klondike gold discovery. Imagine the luck of those men? These newcomers to the North had been planning to head farther downriver to Circle City, Tanana, and Birch Creek areas—where they'd heard there were smaller gold discoveries. That they happened to be in that Forty Mile bar when the gold rush began was a fluke.

Their timing aside, these men were largely mining novices and none was acclimatized to the northern wilderness and weather. Experienced Sourdoughs like Johnny and Skiff knew exactly what to do: they began buying up pieces of claims held by the first cheechakos of the Klondike Gold Rush and others willing to sell. "Many of the newcomers wanted to sell out their holdings and get out of the country," Johnny writes. "They held good ground, but they had no money to buy provisions with, and together with the cold weather, they became disgusted with the country."

These two Sourdoughs could see opportunity as sure as they could smell baking bread. "After some deliberation on our part, we bought interests in about a dozen claims," Johnny recounts. He and Skiff pooled financial resources. Their partnership worked well: Johnny, though not the most social, had an engineer's mind and business acumen; Skiff possessed the gift of gab and knew how to negotiate so everyone felt like a winner. Perhaps most importantly, neither man ever shied away from hard work and each was seriously infected with gold fever, or as the world would soon come to call it, Klondicitis.

January to May 1897 were incredibly busy months for both Johnny and Skiff. They bought more provisions like lumber, nails, and tools at sky-high prices. Shovels and picks were $20 each and a pound of nails $5 (the equivalent of $600 and $150 today). They got to work building a single cabin, sluice boxes, flumes, and dams. They started fires each night to "burn to the bedrock," digging out the unfrozen pay dirt and setting it up for spring cleanup when the water would move the pay dirt through dams and sluice boxes until the gold appeared, separated from the dirt and gravel.

Johnny estimated that it cost them $150,000—on top of what they paid for the claims—to get their operation up and running in the first part of 1897. Again, $150,000 would be equivalent to $4.5 million today. "I still mourn," Johnny laments, "having to leave 10,000 to 11,000 feet of perfectly good whipsawed lumber, when we left Chicken Creek, never to return."

26 ABOVE BONAN...

Reading between the lines, the notion of time clearly changed in Johnny's mind. Where before he described time as "endless" during the long, cold, dark Yukon winters, now time was of the essence. Instead of returning to retrieve all that lumber, Johnny and Skiff were willing to pay exorbitant prices for supplies through the winter to be ready for spring cleanup.

It was all about risk. Everything was on the line, and Johnny was all in. He didn't know how much gold they would find when the rivers and creeks thawed and started running in May. Despite all the perils—immense physical hardship and possible financial ruin—Johnny faced it all in the pursuit of gold.

For almost forty years, I worked next to Ted Rogers, one of the biggest risk-takers in Canadian business history. Author Peter C. Newman called Ted "a riverboat gambler." And Ted did have an amazing appetite for risk. Three or four times, I watched him make bets that almost bankrupted Rogers Communications Inc. It all worked out, and the company reached "investment grade" quality before Ted died in 2008.

But who took greater risk: Johnny or Ted? Johnny was in a "foreign" place, living and working in unbearable conditions. Ted risked his company and family legacy; Johnny risked his life and every cent he'd ever saved.

In the end, I suppose it doesn't really matter. They were both incredible entrepreneurs. And both men, along with my father, Jed Lind, were the strongest male influences of my life.

It is appropriate, albeit coincidental, that when my grandfather started St. Marys Cement a decade after the Klondike, John Grieve Lind (as he was then called) would partner with Alfred Rogers, a first cousin of Ted Rogers's father.

During this early period of buying up claims, Johnny Crist is not mentioned in Johnny Lind's journal. Crist was a partner, but he may not have had the financial resources to be a full partner with Johnny and Skiff. At one time or another on various properties, Johnny also had other associates—Bill Wilkinson, Conrad Dahl, Frank Dinsmore, and others—whom he neglects to mention here too. But Skiff, and to a lesser degree Crist, were his main partners.

Two of Johnny and Skiff's dozen Klondike holdings are worth discussing in more detail. The first was known as 26 Above Bonanza, and "26 Above" became synonymous with Johnny Lind over the years. On Bonanza, this land was twenty-six claims up the creek from Discovery staked by George Carmack. As each claim measured five hundred feet, 26 Above sat thirteen thousand feet (2.6 miles) beyond the Discovery claim.

Typically, "Above" claims were considered lesser than "Below" claims because the flow of water carried gold fragments downstream. But that rule was not set in stone. Undeterred, Skiff and Johnny bought half of 26 Above in January 1897 for $12,000—the equivalent of $360,000 today. (Bill Wilkinson, a miner they knew from their Franklin Gulch days, came in with Johnny and Skiff for a piece, but he sold that back to them in September 1899.) Imagine young men betting all that money for *a chance* at finding gold? The two also bought 1 Eldorado on nearby Eldorado Creek for an undisclosed amount.

These were their headquarters, as it were, on the two creeks. Johnny worked Bonanza investments, and Skiff did the same on Eldorado. By spring 1897, the Sourdoughs had hired two hundred labourers and worked two shifts a day paying $20 per man. Their payroll was an astounding $4,000 per day. (By way of comparison, constables of the North-West Mounted Police earned $1.25 a day, and they worked long and hard to maintain law and order. Women who worked in the dance halls and brothels also worked long and hard, and they earned multiples more than the police and the miners.)

By early spring 1897, 26 Above was yielding some gold, then some more, and more again. Over one twenty-four-hour period in June 1897, the two shifts of workers pulled out "over $50,000 in gold dust and nuggets," Johnny writes, adding that was an extraordinary day, not at all usual. "The returns at times, from our operations, were enormous and at other times hardly anything, but mostly we were quite fortunate."

The original owner of 26 Above, Bernhard Anderson of Sweden, offered to sell Johnny and Skiff the second half for $200,000—up from $12,000 for the first half. At the prospect of harping too much about risk, that is $6 million today for the other half! Skiff and Johnny agreed to the hefty price on February 11, 1898, so long as it was not payable until mid-August. The two of them—and their paid employees—worked their tails off through June, July, and August to reap enough gold to pay for the full claim.

Also worth highlighting is their 1 Eldorado claim. In his landmark book *Klondike*, Pierre Berton gives props to Skiff for buying 1 Eldorado "for a trifle," before anyone really knew how much gold was there. Together, Johnny and Skiff bought the claim from an old Yukon prospector named Jay Whipple. At point of purchase, Johnny, Skiff, and Whipple did not know that each claim on Eldorado would produce a minimum of $500,000 worth of gold, and some a lot more than that. Whipple was no greenhorn so I suspect Berton's "trifle" is, like so much Klondike lore, somewhat hyperbole, especially when they paid $12,000 for *just the first half* of 26 Above around the same time.

"The purchaser [of 1 Eldorado], a lumberman from Eureka, California, named Skiff Mitchell, lived for half a century on the proceeds," writes Berton, a decade after Johnny Lind's death. Tappan Adney also writes about "Old Man" Whipple selling 1 Eldorado to Skiff and his unnamed partner for "a song."

I'd like to think my grandfather is smiling up there because he did not like publicity or being in the limelight, so he would have been fine with Skiff alone receiving Berton's and Adney's accolades. His shyness is also part of the reason that of the hundreds and hundreds of books about the Klondike Gold Rush, old and new alike, my grandfather is mentioned only a handful of times.

For Johnny, the pursuit of gold was all about business and possible fortune, not fame. "Skiff also was doing quite well on Eldorado and every dollar we made, we kept investing in other properties until we were quite large operators," Johnny writes. "By fall [of 1897], I was worn to a shadow, working about twenty hours a day, also doing my own cooking and household duties."

Who were better off, though? The miners who sold out early and cheaply, and returned south or travelled to the next gold rush, or the others who stuck with it, enduring the harsh conditions and back-breaking work?

Johnny Lind, Skiff Mitchell, and about fifty other miners eventually knew when to leave with their Klondike fortunes, and they were definite winners. But for hundreds of other miners, that wasn't the case. Many with incredible amounts of the precious metal blew their newfound wealth thinking that gold was a renewable resource. So many died broken and penniless, such as Big Alex McDonald, the King of the Klondike, and a host of others. As Pierre Berton points out, "If there was conspicuous wealth, there was also conspicuous waste."

Johnny Lind most certainly had a strong opinion on the power—both for good and evil—that immense newfound wealth can have on the human spirit.

FEW LEFT WITH A FORTUNE

The flamboyant characters of the Klondike lived large and took wild risks like betting $50,000 worth of gold on one hand of poker or did obscenely lavish things like bathing in champagne. They are the ones most remembered in literature because their stories are the most entertaining. In essence, strike it rich, live lavishly, and die penniless.

Johnny Lind was not one of those characters. He lived in a cabin near his gold-mining operations, stuck to his knitting, and got the job done. There were others who did the same—the non-ostentatious folks of the Klondike. In many ways, they were kindred spirits to Johnny Lind. Two of their stories stand out from the others.

The first is better known than the second. Clarence and Ethel Berry were from California. In 1894, Clarence proposed marriage and then, before the wedding, went north to strike it rich.

Returning to California no wealthier than when he left, Clarence was delighted that Ethel still agreed to proceed with the wedding. Then they headed north together as

a couple in 1896. They were well suited for the task—and lucky.

They arrived at Forty Mile in June 1896, but, at first, prospecting did not go well. To supplement their income, Clarence tended bar. He was at work on the fateful evening when George Carmack came in boasting of the great gold discovery that he took credit for. Like others in that Forty Mile bar, Clarence scurried off and staked his claim. Ethel joined him, and the couple worked through the winter, living in a shabby twelve-by-sixteen-foot log cabin with a dirt floor.

The next summer, they headed south to convert gold into cash. When Ethel stepped off the steamship *Excelsior* in San Francisco on July 15, 1897, she did not look like a woman already worth more than $100,000, despite her necklace of gold nuggets. Her worn and tattered dress was held together with Clarence's belt. Reporters dubbed her "The Bride of the Klondike," and the couple's story helped spark the gold rush.

Ethel and Clarence returned to the Klondike in 1898 and mined

in Alaska, too, until returning home. They were cautious with their money. Through careful investments, including California oil, they parlayed their Klondike wealth into much more. In all, they brought out an estimated $1.5 million from the North—the equivalent of $45 million today.

Clarence Berry is described by Pierre Berton as "sober, honest, hard-working, ambitious, and home-loving, and he stayed that way. Of all the original locaters on Bonanza and Eldorado, there is scarcely one other to whom those statements apply." But those words aptly describe Johnny Lind, too, and a man named St. John Atherton.

One of the more fascinating stories in the Phil Lind Klondike Gold Rush Collection is about the formerly enslaved man Atherton, who was freed after Abraham Lincoln issued the Emancipation Proclamation on January 1, 1863. For years, Atherton drifted around the United States doing odd jobs. He ended up in Alaska in the 1890s.

When he heard of the big Klondike strike, he headed to the

Detail of a postcard depicting Dawson City, after 1898. Thousands flocked to the Klondike with dreams of wealth. A few hundred struck it rich, but many squandered their earnings in saloons and gambling halls. RBSC-ARC-1820-11-43-08

Yukon Valley and worked and worked until he amassed at least $30,000 worth of gold. Some reports say it was more than $100,000; regardless, his gold was enough to buy the plantation near Atlanta where he was born and had lived in slavery. After the Civil War, the plantation owner had fallen on hard times and mortgaged the property. Following his death, the plantation owner's daughter lived there alone and in poverty.

The slave owner "was kind to me and his daughter was just like him," Atherton is quoted in newspapers and a book entitled *Big Pan-Out*. "The time is coming when it must be sold if the mortgage is not paid, and then she will have no home. What I want to do is get back to Georgia and buy up that mortgage." He said the daughter could live there for as long as she liked. A record of how the story fully and finally played out could not be found. But Atherton's generosity certainly appears to be a magnanimous gesture.

Of the estimated hundred thousand Klondike stampeders, only forty thousand made it to the goldfields. With almost all the rivers and creeks staked before they got there, only about two thousand found gold and only two hundred found significant amounts.

And only forty or fifty miners were like Clarence and Ethel Berry, St. John Atherton, and Johnny Lind—all managing to leave the North with their Klondike fortune intact and ready to be put to good use.

6

THE STAMPEDE

||||||||||||||||||||||||||||||||||||||||||||||||||||||||||||||||||||||||||||

BEGINS

NEWS OF THE RICHES SPREADS TO THE OUTSIDE WORLD

BY FREEZE UP—which was September 15 in 1897—Johnny Lind's mind turned to things other than work, which he'd been doing for nine months straight, up to twenty hours a day, seven days a week.

FACING PAGE: "On the Way to Klondike: Scene Near the Landing-Stage, Dyea," detail from *The Illustrated London News*, January 29, 1898. RBSC-ARC-1820-33-09

At this point, the outside world was in an irrational rage after the first ships with Klondike gold and newly rich passengers arrived in San Francisco and Seattle in July 1897. Amid economic depression and joblessness, the Klondike gold story covered front pages of newspapers everywhere, every day.

Thousands of dreamers were now either on their way or making plans to get to the Klondike. It would be an adventure of a lifetime that could make them rich. Little did they know that they'd be late to the party and if they did make it all the way to the goldfields, they'd likely be working for Johnny Lind and other owners of staked claims.

Among the droves who set out for the Klondike were lawman Wyatt Earp, boxing promoter George "Tex" Rickard, and other public figures chasing a last hurrah, along with teachers, bank tellers, seamen, formerly enslaved men—even a mayor.

The story of William Wood, an attorney, land speculator, electric trolley line president, and then-mayor of Seattle, exemplifies the impetuous gold frenzy. Mayor Wood was at the annual Christian Endeavor convention in San Francisco when on July 14, 1897, the steamship *Excelsior* arrived with its Klondike gold. Two days later, the *Portland*, with its ton of gold, landed in Seattle. (The brief Klondike Gold Rush yielded some 625 tons of gold!)

In today's world with instant messaging, social media, and more, it is almost incomprehensible that such a huge gold strike could remain unknown about for exactly eleven months. But that's what happened from August 1896 to July 1897. And when word got out, the world caught gold fever. Wood's irrational behaviour is just one example of the frenzy that ensued.

Seeing an opportunity to ferry miners and freight from San Francisco and Seattle to the goldfields, Wood immediately wired investor friends in Seattle. They swiftly formed a partnership called the Seattle and Yukon Trading Company. Before the end of July, the corporation chartered the steamship *Humboldt* and placed display ads in the Seattle and San Francisco dailies for the $300 passage to Alaska. Wood then wired Seattle's city hall and resigned as mayor so that he was free to head north.

Wood certainly wasn't alone either. Streetcar operators quit mid-run. Store clerks turned away from customers and walked out of shops. John McGraw, president of the First National Bank of Seattle, jumped at the chance to sail to Alaska on *Portland*'s return voyage. A man with terminal lung disease also boarded the *Portland* and from the gangplank shouted to relatives that he would "rather die trying to get rich, thank you!"

The outside world was feverish and frenetic about the Klondike. Perhaps it was similar to today's social media phenomenon of FOMO—fear of missing out. But in the late nineteenth century, the fear was of missing out on the Klondike riches and adventure. Meanwhile, in the Klondike, Johnny Lind was finally catching his breath—he had no idea that a tsunami of humanity was rolling north, and the newcomers had no idea of the dangers and agonies ahead.

Front Street, Dawson City, July 1899. In a matter of a few short years, between 1896 and 1899, Dawson City's population exploded to around 17,000—and shrunk to about 8,000 after the rush ended. RBSC-ARC-21-10-PAGE-71

From July 1897 onward, between spring thaw and autumn freeze, the wealthy sailed around Alaska to St. Michael and up the Yukon River to the Klondike. However, especially with North America in a deep depression in the 1890s, most people landed at either Skagway or Dyea, two ports on the Alaskan panhandle. These pop-up towns were nine miles apart and now jammed with transients staring at the granite mass of the Coast Mountains, just several miles inland.

Skagway fed the Dead Horse Trail, a twenty-mile march to White Pass. From Dyea, new arrivals took the Chilkoot Trail fifteen miles to Chilkoot Pass. Once over either pass, a Klondike-bound traveller had six hundred more miles to go.

In Skagway, a young opportunist from Oakland named Jack London described tents, huts, and crude wood structures lining muddy streams functioning as streets. He noted sex workers plying their trade in public. Jovial laughter, sometimes frightening screams, and gunfire filled the air. Murder and mayhem abounded in Skagway. Jefferson "Soapy" Smith and his gang of con artists, thugs, and thieves unofficially ruled. One penniless German immigrant who never actually made it to the goldfields started his family's fortune around Skagway, Dyea, and the trails inland. His name was Friedrich Trump, grandfather of Donald Trump, and he amassed his money with a network of brothels, hotels, and gambling saloons near frontier mining towns.

Dead Horse Trail, considered a less punitive route, got its name from the fate of pack animals succumbing to beatings, exhaustion, and falls. That first summer, some forty thousand people hoofed it over Chilkoot Trail and Pass (and its shorter but steeper thirty-three-mile route) and White Pass (longer at forty-five miles) to get to Lindeman and Bennett Lakes, from which the Yukon River ran two thousand miles north and west to the sea, its flow peppered with harrowing rapids.

Meanwhile, the world was on the move, and Johnny could finally slow down a wee bit and build nicer cabins for his men and kick back and read for pleasure, something he'd been unable to do since arriving in the North more than three years earlier. With operations at 26 Above and 1 Eldorado up and running rather smoothly, Johnny moved to 30 Above and Skiff to 18 Eldorado to personally improve production on those lots. "Now we had more comfortable cabins, better food, coal oil lamps instead of candles for light, and I did enjoy the winter of '97 and '98," he writes.

For a modest man, Johnny uncharacteristically pats himself on the back. "It is with some pride to be able to say that I, too, contributed some share in the opening up and development of this very rich mining camp," he writes, clearly aware that he is in the middle of something big, even historic, that will ultimately fascinate people for centuries. But Johnny was not a typical prospector. He talks of the pleasure he found in reading books like Edward Gibbon's *The History of the Decline and Fall of the Roman Empire* and anything by Thomas Carlyle, Victor Hugo, or Thomas Hill Green.

As a man with only an eighth-grade education, Johnny undoubtedly hired a tutor who introduced him to eclectic authors—novelists and biographers, philosophers and scientists. The tutor would either read to Johnny or help him with word pronunciations and concepts explored by these great writers. One thing is certain: Johnny had a thirst for knowledge, not a hunger for Dawson-style entertainment in the saloons and brothels.

He relished his off-hours and rarely went into town, preferring the company of books: "I never in all my life had a chance to read just what I wanted to." Such was the life of a self-made man who had to read books to teach him the skills needed to build railroad bridges or to placer mine for gold, or, years later, to make cement. "What gave me more pleasure than anything else," Johnny confides, "was not being forced to entertain other mine owners or being entertained by them."

Johnny was by no means a hermit, as his numerous partnerships attest. Pure loners cannot work that well with others. He'd also play the odd game of poker in his cabin with visitors. Rarely, though, did he venture the ten miles into Dawson City. And when the tiny community of Grand Forks, at the junction of Bonanza and Eldorado Creeks, was established in the fall of 1897, he'd cash in his gold at a bank branch there, thus further avoiding Dawson and all its shenanigans.

Not even a year old, Dawson was quickly growing into the most populated city west of Winnipeg in Canada. Many, such as local businessman Joe Ladue, were calling it "the Paris of the North." International newspapers picked up on that moniker. The Klondike legend and news of massive amounts of gold travelled North America across telegraph lines and over the seas to the rest of the world. "There was all sorts of entertainment during the winter of '97 and '98," Johnny writes. "Dance halls, gambling joints, two theatres, drinking saloons galore." It cost $1 for a dance, $1 for a shot of watered-down booze, $65 for an "indifferent" bottle of champagne, $8 to $12 for a less-than-tasty dinner, and $2 for an outside newspaper that was a month old. Remember, use a factor of thirty to get an equivalent price today: $300 for a lousy meal, $2,000 for a bottle of cheap champagne, $60 for an old newspaper.

Johnny observed that too many successful mine owners spent most of their time in town, returning to their claims only when they needed gold to pay for their excitement. In town, three things quickly separated miners from their fortunes: booze, gambling, and women.

For many in the Klondike, the real money was in mining the miners, not in panning for gold. Johnny was well aware of this. "Too much sudden wealth went to a great many men's heads and ruined them forever," Johnny writes. "I could name dozens and dozens of fine men in adversity, with fine principles, utterly ruined by a little brief wealth and usually they put on all the airs of a Prince of Blood, while it lasted."

The Phil Lind Klondike Gold Rush Collection at UBC is filled with such stories in hundreds of books. And Johnny Lind would have known nearly every person in each one, both on the climb up and the crash down. Some he knew well and mentions in his unpublished memoirs. He expresses genuine empathy but also tells it like it is, straying from the Klondike myths.

"WHERE WE GOT OUR START."

H.C.

For example, there's the story of Charlie Anderson, nicknamed the Humpback Swede, who worked for Johnny Lind for a brief time in Alaska. In Forty Mile, two Americans got Charlie really drunk in a saloon one night and sold him what they thought was a worthless claim, for all the money he had left in his pocket, which happened to be $600 ($18,000 today).

When he was sober again, Anderson was furious and sought to redress the injustices imposed upon him. When the authorities did not help, in his frustration, Anderson went to the claim, put down a shaft—and found some of the richest pay dirt on the Eldorado. In all, he pulled out $1 million worth of gold, which would be about $30 million today. His nickname then became the Lucky Swede.

Charlie bought a large cabin in Dawson, routinely bathed in champagne, and spent lavishly on himself and others. Eventually he married a dance hall girl who took most of the money he had and left him penniless. By this point he had lost the Lucky Swede nickname. "Poor Charlie went to work in a sawmill," Johnny writes. "There was probably 75 percent of all the wealth taken out of the Klondike that was dissipated in a similar way."

Beyond trickery and cons, another scourge for many miners was gambling, which filled so many dark, cold winter days and nights. Johnny mentions a man who people called "The Pope." He lost $57,000 ($1.7 million today) on one hand of poker. Tex Rickard, who would one day gain fame promoting boxing matches and owning the original Madison Square Garden in Manhattan, cashed out his Bonanza claim for $60,000

($1.8 million today) and used the money to open the Northern saloon in Dawson. At the poker table one night, he lost every cent—and the saloon!

Most gambling losses were for lesser amounts, but there were about two thousand people in Dawson "who derived their living—and they appeared to live well—from the proceeds of gambling and trickery," Johnny writes. Indeed, some dance hall girls solicited extravagant gifts from miners, like gowns imported from Paris that cost upwards of $1,500 in Dawson (the equivalent of $45,000 today). In the end, whenever a miner got fleeced, "it all dwindled down to the miner got drunk and gambled the money away and this band of reptiles could get dozens of witnesses to swear to anything." Caveat emptor!

Beyond the rascals and criminals, the gold also attracted professional gamblers who were on the up-and-up, for the most part. (The crooked gamblers seemed to congregate more in Skagway, out of the Mounties' long reach of the law.) For fifty years, professional gamblers travelled across North America from one gold rush to another. These nineteenth-century folks lived by the twentieth-century catchphrase "follow the money"—and they weren't going to miss the granddaddy of gold rushes.

Harry Woolrich, from Owen Sound, Ontario, was one such gambler. Woolrich will be no stranger to any researcher delving into the Phil Lind Klondike Gold Rush Collection at UBC. His time in the Klondike has been romanticized in many books and by several authors. His exploits at the Dawson City Monte Carlo dance hall and saloon are legendary. Beyond his skills at the card table, Woolrich is known for tragedy and misfortune.

First, the tragedy. He was sharing a room with nineteen-year-old Myrtle Brocee over Silent Sam Bonnifield's famous Bank Saloon and Gambling House in Dawson. Myrtle was a singer and dancer at the Tivoli theatre and dance hall. In "a fit of despondency" after an argument with Harry, Myrtle shot herself in the head using a .32 calibre Smith & Wesson pistol. Pierre Berton writes in *Klondike*: "The coroner's inquest into her death was marked by an odd gallantry: half a dozen men took the stand to testify that they had been sleeping with Miss Brocee. But each blandly swore under oath that, though he had shared her bed, she remained virtuous to the end … [even] Woolrich testified with a straight face that his bed companion was a virgin."

Myrtle, her honour preserved by defenders of Dawson's demi-monde, received a fine burial in an expensive coffin with silver-plated handles. Dozens and dozens of mourners wept at her graveside.

Following this tragedy, Woolrich went from bad luck to fortune to self-inflicted misfortune. With poker, he was having no luck with his own money, and he needed others to "stake him" to play. He was "quite successful, if playing with someone else's money," writes Johnny Lind, "but when playing with his own, he always lost."

The more timid poker players figured they had a better chance of winning by staking Woolrich than by playing their own cards. The man had an aura about him. He had a magic touch. Rubberneckers would stand five or six deep around him just to watch him play.

With sessions routinely going twenty-four to thirty-six hours, meals would be served to him at the table.

Johnny writes, "One night, he cleaned up $70,000 at poker. By the rules of the game, when one staked another, half the winnings went to the man that staked him and the player got the other half." With his $35,000 share of the winnings (more than $1 million in today's money), Woolrich declared an end to his gambling. He was going home to Owen Sound to visit relatives and purge this addictive ill from his body. He bought a ticket on the next steamer out of Dawson. Once he reached Vancouver, he planned to hop on the transcontinental train and head east.

He never made it. The boat was delayed, so he went over to the Monte Carlo to wait and have a drink. "He put $10 on the high card," Johnny says, reiterating that he was not the same player when *his* money was on the table instead of staked money from others. Adds Pierre Berton: "Twenty-four hours later he was still in the same spot, the boat long since gone. When his money ran out, he pulled out the steamer ticket and flung it on the table. And he lost that, too."

Johnny also knew "Swiftwater" Bill Gates (no apparent relation to Microsoft founder Bill Gates), who was an American frontiersman and fortune hunter, and a fixture in so many Klondike stories. He made and lost several fortunes, and he died in Peru in 1935, while pursuing a silver strike at age seventy-five.

Swiftwater's more prominent Klondike stories always involve women. To impress one woman, he bought every egg in Dawson for three dollars each, or $2,500

worth of gold dust. Further smitten, Swiftwater then presented a dance hall girl, Gussie Lamore, with her weight in gold—about $30,000 worth. She took the money but rejected his marriage proposal. Out of spite, Swiftwater married Gussie's sister, Grace Lamore, who also worked in the dance hall. Grace took him for thousands, too, and dumped him after only a few months. He later married Bera Beebe, with whom he fathered two sons, Clifford and Frederick. Unaware Bera was pregnant with Frederick, Swiftwater left Clifford in Dawson with the baby's grandmother, Lola Beebe, and headed south with Bera for a holiday.

This time, Swiftwater did the dumping and subsequently abandoned Bera for fifteen-year-old Kitty Brandon, his niece. Bera, Clifford, and Freddie ended up living in a small Seattle apartment with Lola while Swiftwater travelled the world in search of another fortune.

———

I have a hunch Johnny Lind would have held only disdain for a character like Swiftwater.

I sometimes like to imagine my grandfather interacting with these larger-than-life characters of Klondike lore. Did he ever get in a row with Belinda Mulrooney

as so many others did? Even though he wasn't Catholic, did he ever pray with the diminutive, big-hearted Father William Judge? Did he actually witness someone losing $50,000 in a hand of poker or just hear stories?

My parents told me Johnny often spoke reverently about the Anglican bishop William Bompas, a Cambridge University graduate who could read the Bible in English, Greek, Hebrew, and Syriac. He also spoke of John Pringle, a Presbyterian minister who brought the word of God out to the miners and lived at Gold Bottom Creek.

My grandfather seemed to know everybody I've read about in the Klondike.

Another story wrapped in Klondike lore involves Frank Dinsmore, an old prospector who came north in the early 1880s and whose life was glamorized in books and by Jack London, who featured him in his story "The Gold-Hunters of the North," published in the July 1903 edition of the *Atlantic*. London waxes in the piece:

> Frank Dinsmore is a fair sample of the men who made the Yukon Country. A Yankee, born in Auburn, Maine, the *Wanderlust* early laid him by the heels, and at sixteen he was heading west on the trail that led "farther north." He prospected in the Black Hills, Montana, and in the Cœur d'Alene, then heard the whisper of the North, and went up to Juneau on the Alaskan Panhandle. But the North still whispered, and more insistently, and he could not rest till he went over Chilkoot, and down into the mysterious Silent Land. This was 1882, and he went down the chain of lakes, down the Yukon, up the Pelly, and tried his luck on the bars of Macmillan River. In the fall, a perambulating skeleton, he came back over the Pass in a blizzard, with a rag of a shirt, tattered overalls, and a handful of raw flour.

> But he was unafraid. That winter he worked for a grubstake in Juneau, and the next spring found the heels of his moccasins turned toward salt water and his face toward Chilkoot. This was repeated the next spring, and the following spring, and the spring after that, until, in 1885, he went over the Pass for good. There was to be no return for him until he found the gold he sought.

> The years came and went, but he remained true to his resolve. For eleven long years, with snowshoe and canoe, pickaxe and goldpan, he wrote out his life on the face of the land. Upper Yukon, Middle Yukon, Lower Yukon,—he prospected faithfully and well. His bed was anywhere. The sky was his coverlet. Winter or summer he carried neither tent nor stove, and his six-pound sleeping-robe of Arctic hare was the warmest thing he was ever known to possess. Rabbit tracks and salmon bellies were his diet with a vengeance, for he depended largely on his rifle and fishing tackle. His endurance equaled his courage.

Thanks to the Klondike gold, fortune finally arrived. With his money and feeling a job well done, Dinsmore decided it was time to leave and return to the outside world after fifteen years. "And his own end was as fitting as that of his quest," London writes.

Illness came upon him down in San Francisco, and his splendid life ebbed slowly out as he sat in his big easy-chair, in the Commercial Hotel, the "Yukoner's home." The doctors came, discussed, consulted, the while he matured more plans of Northland adventure; for the North still gripped him and would not let him go. He grew weaker day by day, but each day he said, "To-morrow I'll be all right." Other old-timers, "out on furlough," came to see him. They wiped their eyes and swore under their breaths, then entered and talked largely and jovially about going in with him over the trail when spring came. But there in the big easy-chair it was that his Long Trail ended, and the life passed out of him still fixed on "farther north."

I wonder if my grandfather simply didn't cross paths with the great Klondike chroniclers like Jack London and Tappan Adney. If he had, surely some of his tales would have been used by them? We do know he wouldn't have met Robert Service, the Bard of the Yukon, who penned the poetry book Songs of a Sourdough. *Service arrived in Dawson five years after my grandfather returned home for good.*

Johnny Lind may well be an unknown Sourdough, but he was well known to all who were there during the gold rush.

Jack London sure could paint a picture with his words. Johnny Lind's picture of Frank Dinsmore and his demise is a little different. Calling Dinsmore "one of my old friends and one-time partner... without a doubt the strongest and most powerful man I ever knew with a most pleasing personality," Johnny writes that Dinsmore told him that, after so many years, he "needed out"—he wanted to see the world and had to get out of the Klondike before the freeze-up in the fall of 1897.

Comparing Dinsmore to others that let instant wealth ruin them, Johnny writes that Dinsmore left Dawson with $20,000 in his pocket ($600,000 in today's cash) and proceeded to move from one drunken bender to another, sometimes landing in jail for a spell or two. "He entered every sort of dissipation known and unknown and had to borrow money to get back to Yukon. He arrived back in Dawson a total wreck of a man. When he went out in the Fall he weighed about 250 pounds and when he arrived back he weighed 165 with about every ailment that mortal man could have and live. It was only his determination that kept him alive at all."

Dinsmore was taken to St. Mary's Hospital in Dawson where Father William Judge, the Jesuit priest and founder of the hospital, sent for Johnny, Skiff Mitchell, Harry Spencer, and Bill "Grizzly" McPhee. Spencer and McPhee were co-owners of the Pioneer Saloon and friends and mining partners of Dinsmore. "We had a counsel of war and it fell to my lot to take him out to San Francisco for treatment," Johnny says.

Johnny chaperoned Dinsmore on a riverboat to St. Michael's on the Bering Sea and then an ocean steamer. The trip to San Francisco took twenty-four days, and after two weeks of treatment, Dinsmore insisted that he had to get back to his "beloved mountains."

"We compromised on Denver," Johnny writes. "I stayed there about a week and he appeared to be getting better, but one week after I left him I had a wire from Denver that he was dead."

These stories are cited—particularly the Dinsmore tale—not to embarrass anyone or damage legacies. But rather to remind readers, especially those delving into the full Phil Lind Klondike Gold Rush Collection, that so much myth surrounds that period. Indeed, as Brian Castner points out in his terrific 2021 book *Stampede: Gold Fever and Disaster in the Klondike*, "The most lasting cultural reference to come out of the rush, the Klondike ice cream bar, is literally sugar-coated."

In an odd coincidence, while working on this project, my collaborator, Bob Brehl, discovered Johnny Lind is buried less than a hundred yards from Bob's great-grandparents, Martin and Bridget O'Grady, who lived in St. Marys, Ontario, at the same time as my grandfather.

"I wonder if they knew each other?" Bob asked.

"For sure," I said. "In a small town like that back then, everybody knew everybody."

For the most part, we're all connected. We just don't always know how. My grandfather knew all the Klondike characters, and I just have to believe that he intentionally shied away from any publicity.

After leaving Frank Dinsmore in Denver, Johnny made his way to the Lind family farm in Pond Mills, Ontario, in July 1898. He would return to the Klondike in the spring of 1899—accompanied by two of his younger sisters.

AN ALL-CANADIAN ROUTE TO THE KLONDIKE

Arthur Heming, who gained international renown as the "chronicler of the North" for his vivid paintings, was a promoter of the disastrous all-Canadian overland route to the Klondike. And in a strange coincidence, he was a cousin of Gertrude Heming, the woman who became Johnny Lind's wife. In a short book that is part of the Phil Lind Klondike Gold Rush Collection, Heming calls the all-Canadian route, originating from Edmonton, "the inside track" to getting to the Klondike and predicted that stampeders could use it to reach the goldfields in seventy-five days or so.

Almost one thousand people (mostly men) from the around the world set out from Edmonton, Alberta, believing trails and waterways in Canada would deliver them to the promised land. About one in five (fewer than two hundred) made it to their final destination. The others either perished or turned back. No woman reached the Klondike via the all-Canadian route.

There were several overland routes out of Edmonton, and Heming trumpeted the longest at two thousand miles because "paddling is all down stream … and sails should be taken, as there is often a favourable wind for days." In an article picked up by many newspapers, Heming writes, "All you need is a good constitution, some experience in boating and camping and one hundred and fifty dollars."

Joe Ladue republished Heming's article in his ten-cent book entitled *Klondyke Nuggets*. As a founder of Dawson City with many businesses there, it was in Ladue's financial interests to promote the gold rush. Others, however, thought the overland routes ridiculous, reckless, and a ploy by Edmonton merchants to sell supplies.

Heming selected his route based on reports he'd read from the Hudson's Bay Company, which had used the overland paths north for decades. He himself had only travelled 450 miles north of Edmonton—less than a quarter of the route up the Athabasca River to Great Slave Lake over to the Mackenzie River, then north to the Arctic Circle and Fort McPherson, before turning south on the Peel River to the Klondike region.

It could be argued that it was irresponsible to suggest teams of inexperienced men could travel unmarked trails and navigate waterways that seasoned voyageurs and traders, along with their Indigenous guides, had trekked. No matter which overland route was taken, it was a slog. The reasons were many and varied, from some of the roughest terrain imaginable—muskeg, mudholes, and quicksand; thick forest and dense brush—to deep snow in winter, walls of blackflies and mosquitoes in spring, and a never-ending wilderness of unmarked trails.

Like stampeders, the Canadian government believed the gold rush would continue for years. Indeed, a team of North-West Mounted Police set out to blaze a trail in September 1897. They were to collect details of the terrain, especially river crossings where bridges could be built. Nearly dead, the Mounties finally arrived in the Klondike fourteen months later. Incredibly, at one point they had to hack their way through

A group of men with a boat of supplies, 1897. Between Edmonton and the Yukon, two thousand miles of wilderness teemed with ferocious mosquitoes and raging rivers, mudholes and muskeg. RBSC-ARC-1820-PH-0760

several hundred miles of bush and fallen trees with axes and machetes. Their route through the Peace River Valley and northern BC and on the Pelly River to the Yukon River did not turn out to be the overland trail hoped for. Many who attempted the all-Canadian route perished.

In describing these various torturous trails, James Grierson MacGregor, a mid-twentieth-century author and Alberta historian, cites in his book *The Klondike Rush through Edmonton, 1897–1898* a poignant note tacked on a tree above the body of a man who took his own life. "Hell can't be worse than this trail. I'll chance it."

While in his twenties, Arthur Heming organized a party to travel overland, but he bowed out and never attempted the journey to the Klondike. For the art world, it's a good thing he didn't try. Some in that party who went ahead died of scurvy. Known for his paintings of the Great White North, for most of his life Heming worked in only black, white, and yellow tones because of a childhood diagnosis of colour-blindness. But at age sixty, he suddenly and inexplicably

moved to a Technicolor palette that he splashed across his canvases. A contemporary, but not a member, of the Group of Seven, Heming is best known for the surreal and colourful images he painted during the last decade of his life.

Johnny Lind always thought the all-Canadian route a fool's errand. Needless to say, it was a topic of conversation avoided at the dinner table with his wife and Heming in-laws.

7

UNEXPECTED GIFT

EDNA ELDORADO, THE CHRISTMAS MIRACLE

WE'VE GOT TO talk about the Christmas surprise of 1897 for Johnny Lind, Skiff Mitchell, and Bill Wilkinson.

FACING PAGE: **A winter scene on Bonanza Creek, circa 1897.** RBSC-ARC-1820-PH-1747

This Christmas story is recorded in a little-known book published in 1938 called *I Was There: A Book of Reminiscences* by Edith Tyrrell, a rather extraordinary woman whose husband holds an interesting place in Canadian history, too. The story has also been written up in newspapers over the years.

A bit about the Tyrrells. Joseph Burr Tyrrell was a geologist, cartographer, and mining consultant who, in 1884, was the first to discover dinosaur bones and coal in the Canadian Badlands. The Royal Tyrrell Museum of Palaeontology in Drumheller, Alberta, is named in his honour. In retirement, the Tyrrells owned and operated a huge apple orchard in Scarborough, Ontario, on the land now home to the Toronto Zoo.

Edith Tyrrell, founder and first president of the Women's Association of the Mining Industry of Canada, shared her husband's interest in geology. Twice she went to the Yukon during the gold rush, and it was on her first visit that she heard of this story involving Johnny Lind and his pals.

According to Edith Tyrrell, it was a rather uneventful Christmas Eve, with the three men hooking up their dogs to sleighs and travelling ten miles into Dawson City for supplies. But great excitement would occur on their journey back to their cabins on Bonanza and Eldorado Creeks.

More than halfway back, they noticed the dogs struggling with the heavily laden sleds, so they took a short breather. Johnny noticed a faint light coming from what he thought was a deserted cabin. They went to investigate, and as they drew closer they could hear moaning.

"My God, boys!" Johnny exclaimed. "There's a newborn baby! Bill, run back to the sled and get that bottle of brandy."

The weakened, dying young mother inside the cabin had given birth to a baby girl. The boys started a fire in the stove. They tried to give the mother a teaspoon of brandy, "but she was past swallowing, and as they looked she gave a last quivering sigh and was gone," Tyrrell writes.

The three Sourdoughs took the baby from the dead woman's arms, and Wilkinson wrapped the child in soft woollen underwear. They then lined a packing box with newly purchased blankets to create a makeshift bassinet.

Just then, the husband arrived with a doctor from Dawson. Having looked for help for hours in extreme -45°F cold, and now seeing his dead wife, the man collapsed and died. It was pleurisy, or lung infection, the doctor said. The couple was from the American Midwest; months earlier they had headed out on their Klondike adventure unprepared for the North.

The doctor quickly explained to the three miners about how and what to feed the baby and how to keep her warm, and then he departed for another call.

Johnny, Skiff, and Bill headed back to their cabins with bassinet and baby. "Never had so strange a load gone along the Eldorado trail, or any trail for that matter, as went that Christmas Eve," writes Tyrrell. "The dog team, the three men and the baby, while the northern stars shone brightly on their pathway." Once back home, the men took shifts through the night, holding

the sleeping baby and feeding her teaspoons of tinned milk, warm water, and brandy when she awoke.

On Christmas morning, word spread along Eldorado and Bonanza Creeks of this miracle child. Sixteen women miners arrived, offering help. A Nova Scotian named Mrs. Brock, who had ventured to the Klondike with her husband after their own infant died, took charge while Johnny, Skiff, and Bill began collecting gold dust from miners. Their initial collection amounted to $400, and it was sorely needed: a pint of milk in Dawson cost two dollars. The baby was christened Edna Eldorado, and she brought joy to many that

Klondike Christmas. And the story of "how Bill, Skiff, and Johnny had been led by the Christmas star to the place where the young child was" became folklore.

———————

This story holds obvious parallels to the original Christmas story and underlines the goodness in humanity, especially amid adversity. It's amazing what these three wise men did for that baby, and it makes me— and all my family—proud to be descendants of a man like Johnny Lind.

Of course, if the birth and life of Edna Eldorado were a movie, it would have a Hollywood happy ending. Real life, however, is seldom that simple.

Johnny, in his unpublished memoir, says that over the next few months the miners all tossed in enough gold to purchase a house in Edmonton and set up a housekeeper to look after the child. "The housekeeper, sometime later, took the gold and the girl," writes Johnny. "No one has heard of or seen them since." One can only hope that the housekeeper loved the girl as her own and Edna Eldorado had a long and happy life.

The next Christmas, 1898, Johnny would be in Pond Mills, Ontario, at the family farm. In the spring of 1899, he returned to the Klondike with two of his sisters, Adah and Wilhelmina. The sisters, both steeped in wanderlust like their older brother, were always interested in Johnny's adventures and wanted to see for themselves what he was doing in the Klondike. They had altruistic reasons for the northern trek too: One was interested in teaching and the other nursing. Each wanted to help out. Ultimately, Wilhelmina would end up marrying Skiff Mitchell in 1900, and Adah would marry Johnny Crist in 1902.

The three Linds would have arrived in the Klondike mere days after the huge Dawson City fire of April 26, 1899, oft-times referred to as the unofficial end of the Klondike Gold Rush. Fire was the greatest threat to the town. Dawson was made of wood and canvas and was built in a hurry. Its buildings, cabins, and tents were heated with primitive wood stoves, and they were lit by candles and coal oil lamps.

Together, these were a recipe for disaster, and fires regularly broke out in Dawson. In February of 1899, fire destroyed nine buildings, but the worst inferno erupted in April, when the temperature was forty-five degrees below zero. It started in a bedroom above the Bodega Saloon at 223 Front Street and it quickly spread to the Tivoli theatre north of the Bodega and the Northern saloon to the south, and then it spread to other buildings as firefighters slowly burned a hole in the ice to melt the frozen surface so river water could be pumped to the scene. Incredible as it seems, 110 buildings were destroyed, including the entire business district. The financial loss from that one fire was estimated at $4 million—or $120 million today, for a "city" only two years old. Newcomers' initial impressions of the place were always the same. Dawson City was a misnomer; they expected a metropolis, but found only a camp.

It was around this time that word came of a big gold strike in Alaska, and most prospectors bugged out of the Klondike and headed west 775 miles to Nome. Johnny, his sisters, and his partners stayed near Dawson for a couple more years.

With the new century came the arrival of the huge gold-mining companies and their heavy machinery. That spelled the departure of Johnny Lind, who could see the writing on the wall: smaller operators couldn't compete against the likes of Solomon Guggenheim's Yukon Gold Company, which, with government help, bought up claims and churned through the creeks and rivers with large floating dredges.

EXTRAORDINARY WOMEN OF THE KLONDIKE

The Klondike of the 1890s was a male-dominated world, with an estimated 5 percent of the population of stampeders being women (fewer than two thousand in total). In an era before they were allowed to vote and when work options outside the home were limited, women headed north in search of adventure. Stories of their ingenuity, courage, and confidence abound.

Of course, well before the stampede, Indigenous women such as Satejdenalno (Katherine McQuesten), Neehunilthnoh (Margaret Mayo), and Seentahna (Jennie Bosco) married early explorers, traders, and trappers and shared essential survival skills as well as aided in guiding and interpreting for their partners. They managed to straddle two world views, multiple languages, and complex trading relationships to help their partners succeed, often while raising many children and experiencing extreme changes to their land and culture. Then there was Shaaw Tláa (Kate Carmack), dubbed the "First Woman of the Klondike," who was an integral member of the party that first discovered the gold there; and there was Eliza Isaac (née Harper, the daughter of Chief Gäh St'ät), married to Chief Isaac, chief of the Tr'ondëk Hwëch'in people during the gold rush.

For those who arrived on the scene, "the Klondike held a special attraction for women who believed it was time for the two sexes to stand on a more equal footing. In the chaos and single-mindedness of gold rush society, normal standards were, to some degree, suspended," notes Frances Backhouse in *Women of the Klondike*. There were the likes of Nellie Cashman, the legendary philanthropist and prospector who raised money and gave away hers to charities wherever she mined; and "Klondike Kate" Ryan, the first female special constable of the North-West Mounted Police. There were the pioneering journalists Faith Fenton, Flora Shaw, and Helen Dare. And many, many more.

Terrence Cole, long-time professor of northern studies and history at the University of Alaska Fairbanks, put it best in a PBS television documentary about the gold rush: "The number of women who went on the Klondike stampede wasn't a large percentage. However, those who went seemed to be so much bolder, unfettered, and freer than the men. Not all the men were extraordinary, but all the women certainly were."

Take Martha Purdy, a Chicago socialite from a wealthy family and mother of two young boys when she ventured north in the spring of 1898. Her husband, Will, a son of a railroad president, came home one day overflowing with excitement and declaring his desire to leave his tedious job and join the gold rush. This intrigued Martha, her life filled with endless rounds of theatre, concerts, and tea parties. She was drawn to the adventure and campaigned to join her husband. Her parents supported her and offered to take care of their grandsons.

The couple, along with some friends and Martha's brother, George Munger Jr., boarded a train for the West Coast. At Seattle, Will got cold feet and told Martha he was going to Hawaii instead. He expected her to follow him, but she declined, furious he had decided without talking to her first. She went north without him and never saw Will again.

At the treacherous Chilkoot Pass, with its daunting forty-five-degree climb, thirty-two-year-old Martha made her way into the Yukon, unaware she was pregnant by her estranged husband. After navigating the perilous Yukon River, Martha reached the Klondike. Late to the party with Bonanza and Eldorado Creeks already staked, she ventured to lesser-known Excelsior Creek. Within months, her claims were worth thousands, and Martha employed a crew of sixteen men to work them.

In her little cabin, she gave birth to her third son, Lyman. She also managed the gold-mining operations with her brother, cooked for her crews, and expanded the business to include a sawmill and a gold ore–crushing plant. In 1904, she married a Klondike lawyer named George Black, who became commissioner of the Yukon in 1912

and speaker of the House of Commons in 1930. In 1935, when her husband was ill, Martha ran for and won his Yukon seat as a Member of Parliament. At age sixty-nine, Martha Black became the second woman in Canadian history elected to the House of Commons.

Women like Martha and the most famous Klondike entrepreneur, Belinda Mulrooney, faced incredible obstacles and, with fortitude, seized opportunities. Mulrooney, born in Ireland, arrived in the Klondike via adventures in Pennsylvania, Illinois, California, and Alaska. As luck would have it, she was in Juneau in 1896 when Klondike gold was discovered. At twenty-four years old, she left Alaska and quickly journeyed farther north.

Mulrooney bought merchandise with her savings of $5,000. Her stash included "silk underwear, bolts of cotton cloth and hot water bottles," according to Pierre Berton in *Klondike*. In June 1897 she transported it all across the Chilkoot Pass and on to Dawson City. During the rigorous journey, she wondered if she would be able

to sell such luxury items. Upon arrival, she got her answer from newly rich miners, whose wives paid six times what the goods cost.

Ever the entrepreneur, she built a restaurant in Dawson, and then ventured to the goldfields and established the Grand Forks Hotel, with restaurant and saloon, close to the miners. Second-guessed by men for opening a hotel outside town, she ignored her detractors and it quickly became a roaring success. She started buying mining claims, too, and vowed to construct the finest hotel in Dawson.

Again, doubters laughed. When offered a bet from her most vocal opponent, an old prospector named Bill Leggett, that her grand hotel would not open that summer, Mulrooney accepted. She then smartly and secretly bankrolled bets by her carpenters and other craftsmen so that they had skin in the game. The Fairview Hotel opened its doors on July 27, 1898, with a restaurant and rooms for thirty guests—Leggett paid out $100,000 in lost bets! By age twenty-six, Mulrooney was "the richest woman in the Klondike."

"Panning Out Gold in the Klondyke, Alaska," 1898. The resourceful women of the Klondike participated in all aspects of the gold rush, from owning laundries to running hotels, restaurants, and brothels to mining claims.

8

LEAVING THE KLONDIKE

HOME TO STAY, AND BUILDING ST. MARYS CEMENT

THIS WOULD BE a good time to step back and look at what John Grieve Lind did upon his permanent return to Ontario from the Yukon.

FACING PAGE: An exhausted stampeder, 1900. By 1899, the rush had ended. Johnny Lind left the Klondike in 1901 and returned to Ontario. Mining was becoming more mechanized, and the age of industrial mining was fast approaching. RBSC-ARC-21-10-PAGE-85

First off, it is lost to the Lind Family exactly how much money John Grieve Lind returned home with because he was private when it came to his financial affairs. Certainly, he brought home at least hundreds of thousands of dollars from the Klondike, perhaps even an amount in the low millions. At the 30-to-1 factor comparing today's dollars to 1900 currency, if he returned with $1 million it would be the equivalent of $30 million today.

He and his partners invested great sums buying staked claims and materials, not to mention the whopping $4,000 per day paid out to the miners working their claims at the height of operations. Still, based on government documents, including royalty payments, it is reasonable to surmise that John Grieve Lind brought home more than $200,000—likely significantly more.

Back in Ontario, he did two things immediately: he bought a home for his sisters who were not yet married; and second, he judiciously looked for business opportunities.

It appears he bought three homes for unmarried Lind sisters: one each for Jane (Jennie), Mary (Minnie), and Ellen (Ella Belle). Wilhelmina married Skiff Mitchell in 1900, and Adah married Johnny Crist in 1902, so he likely didn't buy them homes. Sisters Ann, Jessie, Margaret, and Agnes (Aggie) were already married by the time he left the Klondike for good in 1901. His brother, George, had also married in 1900. It says something about the character of the man that after everything he went through to make his fortune, he helped family members with less money. He himself didn't wed until 1905, when he married Gertrude Dagmar Heming.

As for business endeavours, he envisaged a future in cement. That may sound obvious to readers now deep into the twenty-first century, but at the time it took a visionary like John Grieve Lind to bet it all on cement. In 1900, roads were dirt, early skyscrapers were no higher than tall oaks, and our world was a long way from being paved over. But the shrewd Sourdough foresaw an explosion of economic growth coming to North America—and that as the continent quickly became more and more urban, less and less rural, cement would be the backbone of the necessary infrastructure.

First, he invested some of his Klondike money in the Grey & Bruce Cement Company, and soon he became the principal owner of its Owen Sound cement plant. The venture wasn't altogether successful, though, because the plant wasn't equipped to produce a new type of cement developed in England in the mid-1800s called Portland, named for the limestone Isle of Portland in the English Channel. Believing in this new cement, John Grieve Lind and one of his brothers-in-law, A.G. Larsson, a chemist at the Durham Cement Company, started researching and learning everything they could about it.

Once again, in starting St. Marys Cement, my grandfather demonstrated the self-taught aspect of his personality and his dogged determination to succeed.

John Grieve Lind and Larsson decided in 1910 that St. Marys, Ontario, with its abundance of limestone, clay, and water nearby, would be an ideal location for a new factory. It was also situated on two national railway lines, had access to hydroelectric power from Niagara Falls, and was close to the giant US market. Next, John Grieve Lind rounded up investors such as Alfred Rogers, J.P. Bickell, and George M. Gooderham in Toronto.

They called it St. Marys Portland Cement Company Limited. The original plan was to disassemble the Owen Sound plant and move it to St. Marys, but when this proved impractical, construction began on a new plant, costing $250,000 (about $7.5 million today). The plant opened in November 1912, with ninety employees producing 180 tons per day of a product called "Pyramid Brand" Portland Cement—it sold for nine dollars a ton and was an immediate success.

John Grieve Lind, who by this time had married Gertrude Heming of Owen Sound, moved his young family to St. Marys just before the plant's official opening. He was a minority owner and the plant manager, and the only owner to live in the town.

There were other pressures, too, including the dubious business practices of Max Aitken of New Brunswick (later Lord Beaverbrook), and his Canada Cement Company. Aitken had merged eleven cement companies in Quebec, Ontario, and Alberta, often using misleading business practices to achieve his goals. Headquartered in Montreal, his was the largest cement company in the country and, even though Canada Cement also used the Portland system of cement production, John Grieve

Lind refused to sell out to Aitken. Aitken resorted to anti-competitive pricing and threats, but the fledgling St. Marys Cement refused to be intimidated and remained independent.

Indeed, John Grieve Lind and, later, his son John Skiffington Lind, would grow St. Marys Cement into the largest independently owned cement company in Canada.

St. Marys Cement was sold, against my wishes as a minority owner and board member, in 1997.

Over his thirty-five years living in St. Marys, John Grieve Lind became one of the biggest supporters of the community and its institutions. The St. Marys Museum says this: "No one had greater impact on the Town of St. Marys in the 20th Century than John Grieve Lind."

There were no airs about this former Sourdough. A wonderful story that illustrates this involves a Cadillac salesman, who during the Depression was knocking on doors of wealthier people hoping to sell luxury vehicles. The salesman was startled when, after recently returning home from the St. Marys plant, John Grieve Lind opened his front door with cement dust all over his clothes. The salesman looked him up and down, from head to toe, figured he was wasting his time, and was about to leave without even giving his pitch. John insisted on hearing about what the other man was selling.

The fellow gave a tepid sales pitch, cut in half to save time, and turned to leave. Just then the Sourdough-turned-cement-entrepreneur said, "Okay, I'll take two." The salesman's jaw dropped and he was tongue-tied as he scribbled down particulars to fill the order.

John Grieve Lind was also a Freemason who rose to one of the highest ranks; he obtained the thirty-third degree, a supreme honour bestowed only on those who have demonstrated outstanding service to the Masonic brotherhood, as well as professional and personal accomplishments. Only a handful of Canadians have reached this level. A semi-secret fraternal organization, Freemasonry unites "men of good character who share a belief in the fatherhood of God and the brotherhood of mankind," as the Freemason website reads. Famous Freemasons include George Washington, Benjamin Franklin, Franklin D. Roosevelt, Clark Gable, John Wayne, Richard Pryor, Oscar Wilde, Harry Houdini, and Canadians Tim Horton, John A. Macdonald, John Diefenbaker, Bill Davis, and Roy Thomson.

Beyond running the cement plant, the largest employer in the region, and helping to put bread on the tables of hundreds of families, John Grieve Lind was also the father of the St. Marys public parks and recreation system, becoming its first parks commissioner. When the town bought the baseball-diamond lands called "The Flats" (now Milt Dunnell Field, named for the famed *Toronto Star* sports columnist who grew up in St. Marys), he bought property immediately north of The Flats so that he could expand the facility for other sports, including lacrosse and hockey.

"The 3 Spot. White Pass and Yukon Route," after 1897. Around 35,000 men worked on construction of the railway. The last spike was driven at Carcross on July 29, 1900, with crews having worked south from Whitehorse and north from Skagway. RBSC-ARC-1820-PH-0321

A group of people gathered at end of the railway, after 1897. By the time the White Pass and Yukon Route was completed, the gold rush had ended—and demand for the railway's service diminished as prospectors left.

And, during the Depression, John Grieve Lind purchased the seven-acre Cadzow Park on Church Street South, including a century home on the property, and built the Cadzow swimming pool. (On opening day, he sat by the pool and tossed pennies to the bottom so that children could dive for them.) He also donated the property's stone house, which eventually became St. Marys Museum. "He envisioned municipal parkland all along the Thames River and Trout Creek," says Amy Cubberley, the museum's curator. "Although this did not happen in his lifetime, he would have approved of today's system connecting walkways and parks along the waterfront."

One of the best examples of John Grieve Lind's community building was his purchase of derelict lots near his home on Church Street South during the early 1930s—in the depths of the Great Depression—and his turning them into a lovely green space, now called Lind Park. He hired a landscape architect and labourers from the cement plant to do the heavy work such as building the stone walls on the south and west sides with pillared entrances into the park. This brought twofold benefits during the Depression: he provided more hours of work for hungry men and created a lasting beautification for the town at the same time.

In 1942, the year before I was born, my grandfather donated the Lind Park to the people of St. Marys. Our family has continued his legacy over the years by supporting parks and recreation in the town with donations to the development of the Quarry, the tennis courts, the swimming pool, the Lind Sportsplex, and the Canadian Baseball Hall of Fame.

In considering the life of an unsung Sourdough, words from Robert Service sum it up neatly. Service described the bleakness of a Yukon miner's life best in his book of poems entitled *Songs of a Sourdough*—a book that would earn him a fortune greater than most prospectors would ever realize.

> This is the Law of the Yukon, that only the Strong
> shall thrive;
> That surely the Weak shall perish, and only the Fit
> survive.
> Dissolute, damned and despairful, crippled and
> palsied and slain,
> This is the Will of the Yukon,—Lo, how she makes
> it plain!

Obviously, young Johnny Lind was strong and fit, a man who thrived under the will of the Yukon by working extremely hard and avoiding dissipation and debauchery that ruined far too many in the Klondike.

Although Johnny is not as well known as Jack London or Tappan Adney, nor Big Alex McDonald, Belinda Mulrooney, and a host of other Klondike characters, he is the reason the University of British Columbia now holds and safeguards a collection that the Canadian government has designated "a cultural property of outstanding significance."

EPILOGUE

THOUGH MY grandfather Johnny Lind never returned to the North, so many of his descendants have done so over and over, both to experience the beauty of the area and to imagine the hardships our trailblazing ancestor endured so that we would have so much.

In 2001, after the Lind family donated $275,000 to the Dawson City Museum, in part to pay for the John G. Lind Storage Facility and the Lind Gallery, local historian Michael Gates wrote this in the *Klondike Sun*:

> The Lind family is neither new nor unfamiliar to the community of Dawson. They have been actively involved in the centennial celebrations of the past few years, starting in 1996, and continuing to the present. Characteristic of their visits is the energy and enthusiasm they display, and the numbers of the clan who descend upon the community at once. They don't just visit Dawson, they invade, invariably heightening the energy level around town during their stay.
>
> Significant about their involvement with the community has been not only their enthusiasm, but the continuity. It is also rare to find a family so aware of the origins of its good fortune, and a willingness to return that to the community in a meaningful and lasting way. In that regard, the family has set a shining example of philanthropy and generosity, which will be a challenge for others to follow.

My dad, Jed, made five trips to the Yukon and took along members of his family each time. He walked, canoed, drove, and flew to the Klondike, all to capture just a hint of what his father must have gone through.

One memorable trip for me was when I was in my twenties—either during the late 1960s or early 1970s. Together with a classmate from UBC and two of his pals, we rented a couple of inflatable Zodiac boats with small Evinrude motors and journeyed down the Yukon River from Whitehorse, Yukon, to Koyukuk, Alaska, about 1,500 miles.

As the crow flies, Koyukuk is close to the ocean, but in river miles, we were still almost five hundred miles from the Yukon River's mouth at the Bering Sea. At Koyukuk, the Yukon turns sharply south, then west, and finally north where it empties into the Bering.

FACING PAGE: **On the trail to the White Pass, 1899. A man looks out at a river and mountains in the distance, in the stunning landscape of the North.** RBSC-ARC-1820-PH-1186

I suppose I, too, was trying to get a sense of some of the things my grandfather went through during his northern exposure, especially the rapids and canyons along the Yukon from Whitehorse to Dawson. My trip happened long before I started my Klondike collection, but I was certainly already interested in Johnny Lind's great northern achievements because my father, full of pride, would tell me about them many times.

By the time of our trip, the famed Whitehorse Rapids were no more. The Whitehorse Dam, built in 1957 to 1958, submerged the rapids beneath the newly created Schwatka Lake. Still, we went through some harrowing moments at other rapids. It should be noted that the most severe rapids are generally between Whitehorse and Dawson, where the water falls, on average, almost a foot-and-a-half in elevation per mile. From Dawson to the Bering Sea, the Yukon River descends less than one foot per mile on average.

Zodiacs are the type of boat Greenpeace do-gooders made famous by taking them out on the high seas and positioning them between whalers and whales to save the giant mammals. There's no comparison between our Zodiacs and the homemade boats used on the Yukon River during the gold rush. We had motors to make navigating rapids easier; the motors also helped us travel faster, since miners only had paddles, poles, and makeshift sails to propel them. Still, our river journey took six weeks through July and August.

We did get a dose of one thing Johnny Lind and the others went through: bugs. The mosquitoes were so bad, so aggressive, and so annoying that we had to find islands in the Yukon River each evening to make camp. The bugs were so thick on shore that we simply couldn't sleep there. They were still bad, but tolerable, on these little islands.

At the end of our trip, near Koyukuk, Alaska, I saw something that piqued my curiosity. That day in the utterly remote wilderness, after looking endlessly at rocks, trees, and water, I spotted what turned out to be a giant radar dome in the middle of nowhere. While on shore for a break, I climbed over a riverbank to investigate. Out of the blue, I also saw a strange sight: a jet runway more than a mile long carved out of the bush. I called the guys to come have a look. It was extraordinary.

We had stumbled upon a Cold War–era fighter base and radar station known as Campion Air Force Station, where the US Air Force had jet fighters on alert for Soviet Union aircraft and nuclear missiles. No doubt, there were also American nuclear weapons at the ready, too. Calling it a "Cold War" was a misnomer; it was most definitely a hot spot for these military personnel. We later learned that pilots on duty slept in their flight gear so they could scramble and be airborne in less than five minutes. This was a forward fighter base whose pilots rotated into and out of it regularly from the Lower 48, because of its remoteness. (Indeed, we discovered later that air force tours to the base had to be reduced from fifteen months to no more than a year after several studies found the psychological strain and physical hardship too much for most people stationed there.) Calling it a "secret" base may be stretching it, but it was certainly not known well to the public. And

there really was no "public" anywhere close; just wilderness as far as the eye could see.

As we stood there, mouths agape, looking at the runway and base, jeeps came roaring out of nowhere, and Military Police, their guns trained upon us, started asking questions like who we were and what were we doing there. Finding our explanations lacking, they escorted us onto the base and into an interrogation room, where some high-ranking officers grilled us. Initially, they thought we were spies because people simply don't "drop in" on this remote base. I was wearing an old cotton Chicago Black Hawks jersey that was hot and uncomfortable. Sweat began dripping down my brow. Maybe they thought I was nervous; I don't know. But I told them about my grandfather and the Klondike and how we were trying to recapture some of the past.

They mellowed and let us go. But first, they took us to the canteen for some grub and to the PX (post exchange)

where we bought really inexpensive cigarettes and booze. All's well that ends well. We finished our river trip, chartered a civilian airplane out of nearby Galena Air Force Station, and were out of the wilderness for the first time in six weeks! Both those Air Force stations have since been closed down; relics of the potentially dangerous and often highly tense Cold War era.

On another Lind family trip, the *Klondike Sun* again wrote about us:

> Phil Lind talks of the Klondike as if he wants to be laughing all the time he's here, as if he's full of energy and good will for the place. "It's been kind of a tradition in our family," Lind says. "What was told to us was that you could do anything if you set your mind to it, because that's how grandfather did it. I think it's about the spirit of what is encompassed here rather than the actual [fact] that he went and mined for gold. There's a lot of philosophy behind this thing… the spirit of the Yukon, which is that there are opportunities available, but it's not easy. Life isn't easy so you have to work to succeed." That work may be hard, but it has rewards that may be passed on through generations.

Yes, it was passed on through generations. The spirit of the Klondike—hard work, perseverance, big dreams, and humbly giving back when good fortune smiles—never left my grandfather, nor any of us.

Third, fourth, and fifth generations of Johnny Lind's descendants are all going back to the Klondike in 2023,

and I'm proud to say my granddaughter, James, will be twelve years old then—and ready to climb the Chilkoot Pass with some of her Lind relatives, such as cousins and her father (my son), Jed Lind. (My grandson, Jack, will be a toddler in 2023, but he'll likely one day venture over the pass too.) I've climbed it before and cannot anymore, but I always look forward to hearing stories of relatives' experiences!

As for my grandfather, who led us all on this incredible journey that's lasted more than 125 years so far for the Lind family, I marvel at what he endured over those seven years in the North hunting for gold, and I would never claim that I could have replicated what he achieved and withstood. I'm sure all his descendants feel the same way.

Beyond gold and changing the financial fortunes of the Lind family, my grandfather left us much more: a legacy that includes working hard to fulfill big dreams and giving back to communities, and an example of simple goodness and kindness found in the man. I like to think I share some of the qualities and attributes he exhibited over his eighty years: dogged determination and hard work, fierce loyalty and deep friendships, sportsmanship, appreciation of the outdoors and protection of the environment, and, of course, the importance of family.

Johnny Lind, later in life known more formally as John Grieve Lind, was more than an unsung Sourdough. To me, he is an unsung hero who positively impacted so many lives.

ACKNOWLEDGEMENTS

FIRSTLY, I'D LIKE to thank my alma mater, the University of British Columbia, for recognizing the intrinsic value of the Phil Lind Klondike Gold Rush Collection for future generations to enjoy, and for housing and protecting it for years to come. In particular, Katherine Kalsbeek, Michelle Blackwell, Claire Williams, and everyone else involved with UBC's Rare Books and Special Collections. I am also indebted to the Department of Canadian Heritage for designating the collection "a cultural property of outstanding significance."

I would be remiss if I did not highlight the work of Page Two, in particular publisher Trena White; creative director Peter Cocking, for making the book look so good; project manager Rony Ganon; uber-editor Kendra Ward, for her insights and suggestions; and copyeditor Rachel Ironstone. It's also important to mention Allie Winton, a sensitivity editor, who helped us avoid errors of omission and bring to life the crucial roles played by Tagish, Tlingit, and Tr'ondëk Hwëch'in people during the gold rush, and the sacrifices and hardships they endured. Candice Hopkins, through research, the oral tradition, and her writings, further opened my eyes to the importance of Indigenous Peoples to this story. Hopkins is an independent curator, writer, and researcher of the Carcross/Tagish First Nation who predominantly explores areas of Indigenous history and art. She is also a descendant of the true discoverer of Klondike gold as her great-grandmother was a niece of Keish, also known as Skookum Jim Mason.

It's also appropriate to thank friends and colleagues Jan Innes, Missy Goerner, and Michelle Cha for their support and input in helping bring this book together. And my good friend Don Boswell, who, as CEO of PBS's Buffalo affiliate WNED back in 2015, produced the documentary *The Klondike Gold Rush*. His production was the first to highlight and examine the exploits of my grandfather, albeit in a condensed but powerful way, on television. The program aired on all PBS stations across North America and remains available online to view for free.

I'd also like to tip my hat to my co-author and collaborator, Robert Brehl, who, from the very first time I mentioned my grandfather, was fascinated by Johnny Lind's story of courage and perseverance. Bob may not have been the first to suggest a book about Johnny Lind, but he pushed me for at least five years to write about him to help cement my grandfather's little-known Klondike legacy.

I would also like to specially thank my brothers, Ron and Geoff, and sister, Jenifer, all of whom have shared my passion and admiration for what our grandfather did in all aspects of his life. To my first cousin Margaret and her late husband, John King, for taking Grandfather's handwritten notes and journals and meticulously typing them out into readable documents that were enormously important in making Johnny's story come alive in this book.

I am beholden to my late father and mother, Jed and Susie Lind, for introducing me to the Klondike and my grandfather's adventures. Their stories and vivid recollections ignited a fire inside me to build the collection. I also wish to offer a word of thanks to the antiquarians and dealers across North America who helped me tremendously to grow the collection over fifty years. It started as a family passion with my father, and it became something much more.

And lastly, of course, I wish to say John Grieve Lind, who died just before my fourth birthday, was one of the greatest influences of my life. His example has instilled in all Lind descendants a desire to work hard and give back to communities. Quite simply, if not for this humble, warm-hearted man, this book and the collection at UBC would not exist.

PHIL LIND KLONDIKE GOLD RUSH COLLECTION

UBC ALUMNUS and Canadian broadcasting and telecommunications icon Phil Lind donated to the university his collection of rare books, photographs, maps and posters, old newspapers, and valuable and unique ephemera from the Klondike period.

The Phil Lind Klondike Gold Rush Collection, an unparalleled archival collection, was assembled over fifty years and has been designated "a cultural property of outstanding significance" by the federal government's Department of Canadian Heritage. The collection includes more than five hundred books, 1,800 photos, and seventy-four maps, as well as diaries, letters, and other personal items from the estimated forty thousand people who made it to the Klondike in the late 1890s and early 1900s. The donation has been valued at $2.5 million, which includes financial support to ensure it is preserved and made available to the public at the UBC Library, where it will support research and learning.

FACING PAGE: Falls on the White Pass and Yukon Route.
RBSC-ARC-21-10-PAGE-33

ABOUT THE AUTHORS

PHIL LIND is the vice-chairman of Rogers Communications Inc. and for forty years was the right-hand man of the company founder, the late Ted Rogers. Indeed, Lind co-authored (with Robert Brehl) *Right Hand Man: How Phil Lind Guided the Genius of Ted Rogers, Canada's Foremost Entrepreneur*. In 2019, the book was a finalist for the National Business Book Award. A patron of the arts and a philanthropist, Lind holds a steadfast belief that deeper understanding and connection can create a more inclusive world. From revolutionizing the broadcasting landscape in Canada to transforming the potential of telecommunications, his work has greatly contributed to the social, cultural, and economic well-being of Canada. Lind is a long-time supporter and advocate of the University of British Columbia. He has generously invested in many areas of scholarship at the university, including the Phil Lind Initiative, which invites leading US thinkers to UBC for open, thought-provoking dialogue on a range of urgent issues. Lind has also supported the Phil Lind Chair in US Politics and Representation, the US Studies Program, the Rogers Communications Multicultural Film Production Project, and the Belkin Curator's Forum. Lind has been inducted into the Order of Canada and the Cable Hall of Fame in Denver, Colorado. He is also an avid collector of contemporary art, including such Vancouver superstars as Jeff Wall and Rodney Graham. Lind holds a lifelong passion for fly-fishing, passed down to him from his grandfather Johnny Lind.

ROBERT BREHL is an award-winning journalist formerly at the *Toronto Star* and *Globe and Mail*. Brehl now operates his own consulting, communications, and writing firm called abc² communications inc. (abc2.ca). He is co-author of the bestselling books *Relentless: The True Story of the Man behind Rogers Communications*, with Ted Rogers; *Right Hand Man: How Phil Lind Guided the Genius of Ted Rogers, Canada's Foremost Entrepreneur*, with Phil Lind; and *Hurricane Hazel: A Life with Purpose*, with Mississauga's Hazel McCallion, the longest-serving mayor of a major city in Canadian history. Brehl has authored other books, including the bestseller *The Best of Milt Dunnell: Over 40 Years of Great Sportswriting*, about the legendary Canadian sports columnist from St. Marys, Ontario. Like *Right Hand Man*, *Relentless* (2009) was a finalist for the National Business Book Award. Brehl has a book about Calgary oilman and environmentalist David Werklund scheduled for publication in spring 2023.

THE. HOTEL
MAINE.

OTEL MAINE. TAAKENA
LADY COOKS,
ESH FRUIT FISH & GAME
ALWAYS ON HAND,
NORMAN D. MAC   AY PROP.